Managing in a Service-Focused World

I, team, stewards and marketplace

Managing in a Service-Focused World

I, team, stewards and marketplace

ROGER K. WILLIAMS

IT Governance Publishing

IT Governance Publishing
IT Governance Limited
Unit 3, Clive Court
Bartholomew's Walk
Cambridgeshire Business Park
Ely
Cambridgeshire
CB7 4EA
United Kingdom

www.itgovernance.co.uk

First published in the United Kingdom in 2014
by IT Governance Publishing.

ISBN 978-1-84928-684-8

DEDICATION

To my Mom and Dad, for showing me how to live a good life, and to Jennifer, for inspiring me to strive for it.

ABOUT THE AUTHOR

Roger K. Williams has spent 20+ years in retail, 18+ years in IT, and over a dozen years in leadership roles at Fortune 50 companies. In addition to those experiences, he has also earned numerous certifications including ITIL Expert, PMP, COBIT 5 Foundations, HDI Support Center Manager, ISO20000 Foundations, and Toastmasters Advance Communicator Bronze. He has spoken at international conferences and panel sessions on ITSM and navigating the future of computing. His writings on managing attention and harnessing technology trends at the RogertheITSMGuy blog and on Google+ have garnered praise from a diverse audience. Roger resides in North Carolina.

ACKNOWLEDGMENTS

I am grateful to Vicki Utting and the team at IT Governance Publishing for unfailing help and service at every step of the process of creating this book. ITSMF USA's Susan Schellhase provided initial encouragement that was essential in getting started. Thanks also to this book's reviewers, Chris Evans, ITSM specialist and Dave Jones, Pink Elephant. This book is better because of your feedback.

In keeping with the theme of this book, I'd like to thank the people who have helped me along the way in each of my circles:

Marketplace: I have had the pleasure of meeting and learning from great minds in the ITSM industry and in related fields, including Aprill Allen, Matt Beran, Charles Betz, Michael Cardinal, Chris Dancy, Amy Donahue, Troy DuMoulin, Rob England, Karen Ferris, Jon Francum, Majid Iqbal, Mark Kawasaki, Peter Kretzman, Katherine Lord, Joel Pomales, and Jack Probst. My wish is that this book reflects well on them and is as useful to others as their work has been to me.

Stewards: My career has benefited from great leaders. In particular, Lonnie Harrold, Tim Jacks, Tom James, Hank Marquis, Shane Marsh, Nancy Martin, and Joe Pardini have provided guidance, challenges, and support essential to my development.

Team: Some of my important lessons in management have come from my direct reports and peers. I am especially indebted to Michael Davis, Hannah Dowdle, Mechelle Franklin, Brittany Hansgen, Sam Pienkowski, Scotty Rhoades, Frank Skinner, Faye Sturdivant, Marcel Verolme, Eric Welborn, and Dan York. While I have failed all of them more than they deserve, my desire to help them succeed has never faltered.

I: My close friends Anand, Josh, Jason, Dan, Anthony, Cassie and Rodney have always been there for me. My family is my inspiration – Tim, Lisa, Vanessa, Kenda, Jerry, Crissy, Skylar, Cameron, Jenna, and Fonda, you are always close to my heart even when we are far apart.

Mom and Dad have always been kind, firm, and unwavering in their support. While my world is very different from theirs, the lessons I learned from them on the farm have served me well.

Acknowledgments

Two special ladies are my backbone at home. Daisy the ITSM hound dog has been by my side for nearly all of this book's creation, albeit while usually napping. My wife Jennifer's belief in me often exceeds my own. The last 11 years have been more enjoyable than I could have ever imagined, and I can't wait to see what comes next.

CONTENTS

Contents

Contents

INTRODUCTION – MANAGEMENT AS A SERVICE

Management as a profession has never had an impressive reputation. Business thinkers deride management as a poor substitute for leadership. Startups describe management as a distraction from real work. Staff view management as bureaucracy. No one wants to be a manager when they grow up!

Management is not glamorous or glitzy. It is rarely dramatic or exciting, even when done well. Actions only yield results over time, and require patience. So why bother? It is the best tool for organizations to achieve their objectives. Good management provides value and is a competitive advantage. Management is a necessary, even **noble**, profession. It reduces waste and improves results. It also has a huge impact on the happiness (or lack thereof) of those who are managed.

Few people view IT service management (ITSM) as a useful resource for how to manage, despite the name. The word management appears over 7,000 times in ITIL® v3. However, it does not define the term on its own. Nor does it provide specific guidance about the topic.

ITSM thinking applies to management because it is a service. Like all other services, management is judged on how well it meets the needs of stakeholders. A manager's role has four primary stakeholder groups. This book's four parts each focus on one stakeholder group:

1. You (I)
2. Peers and direct reports (Team)
3. Supervisors and other leaders (Stewards)
4. Customers and other external parties (Marketplace)

Each part describes how to apply the thinking behind the service lifecycle and ITSM processes, as well as related knowledge from other fields, to management. Each chapter concludes with specific actions to improve skills and results.

While this book is suitable for anyone, new and aspiring managers will probably reap the most benefit. The transition from individual contributor to manager is the hardest transition to make in today's modern careers. It is overwhelming, and most management advice is useless, at best. While ITSM has an 'ivory tower' reputation in some circles, the ideas in this book have been used, and refined, to help people like you deliver results.

As Eleanor Roosevelt said, 'Learn from the mistakes of others. You can't live long enough to make them all yourself.' Enough talk – time to get started!

PART I: PERSONAL EFFECTIVENESS

'Lack of direction, not lack of time, is the problem. We all have 24 hour days.' – Zig Ziglar

Focus matters. Modern technology is powerful. Distractions are plentiful. Applying the service lifecycle to ourselves enables us to deliver results that matter. It provides the foundation for today's successful manager.

CHAPTER 1: LEVERAGING STRATEGY GENERATION FOR A PERSONAL SUCCESS STRATEGY

'If you know the enemy and know yourself, you need not fear the result of a hundred battles. If you know yourself but not the enemy, for every victory gained you will also suffer a defeat. If you know neither the enemy nor yourself, you will succumb in every battle.' – Sun Tzu

Achievement does not normally happen by accident. It starts with a clear vision of what success looks like. Enterprises invest a lot of time, money, and energy into strategic planning to produce this vision. They value it, and you should too. A good personal strategy can give you clear direction and confidence. Without a personal strategy you will waste time and energy on things that do not matter. You will miss opportunities for meaningful growth. Your dreams may remain nothing more than dreams.

The idea of having to develop a strategy yourself may be scary. Maybe you've never even been in a strategy session. You don't have a team of MBAs. You won't be hosting an off-site meeting in Maui anytime soon. You don't even know where to start! Can ITSM really help?

Yes, it can! ITIL service strategy defines strategy as a plan intended to achieve defined objectives. It recommends a four-step lifecycle approach to develop, and maintain, a strategy known as the four Ps – see *figure 1*.

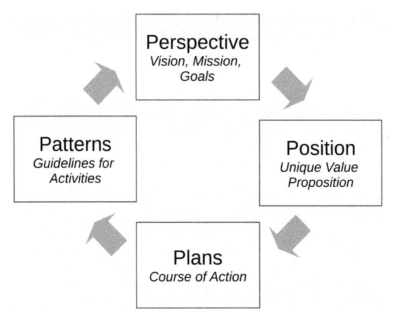

Figure 1: The four Ps of strategy

Let's see how we can apply this lifecycle to create a personal strategy.

Step 1: Determine Perspective

ITIL equates perspective with the vision, mission, and goals of an organization. You may hear people dismiss talk about a personal mission statement, personal brand, etc. as wasted effort. While there are some common pitfalls to avoid, don't neglect this step. It provides focus on the key things that will drive success, while minimizing and/or avoiding items that are not helpful.

Focusing on results is critical to success. Regardless of our intent, others reward or punish us based on our results. Just because a company intends to make a good product, this does not mean people will buy it! Likewise, we have all said things with good intent that we would love to take back. Good intention is not enough. We must also deliver.

There are two types of results of interest: milestones and outcomes. Milestones are oriented around the one-time results of an action, such as payments and products. Outcomes are the changes over time related to our needs, such as improved health and better relationships. Outcomes are like milestones but are broader in scope.

The most common mistake is defining a vision focused on milestones (popularly known as a 'bucket list'). Suppose you define your vision as being a CIO of a Fortune 500 company, having a spouse and two kids, owning a nice house and retiring at age 50. While this is better than no vision at all, there are several drawbacks to a 'milestone' vision:

- It focuses on external decisions that may be out of your control.
- It excludes many other similar visions that may also be fulfilling, such as leading a non-profit company, working at a more enjoyable job until 60, or having more children.
- Even if you somehow achieve this vision, what do you do then?
- It is tempting to let the end justify the means.
- You will spend most (if not all) of your life falling short of this, so you may spend most of your life feeling like a failure.

Worst of all, you might achieve all your milestones and find they didn't really matter to you after all. How can you avoid these issues? One method is to use the '5 Whys' tool, typically used by problem management to understand your true desires. Let's apply it to our prospective CIO:

Why do you want to be a CIO?

- Get rich
- Have the respect of others
- Be able to perform big, ambitious projects that change the world
- Leave a legacy

We can ask 'why' about each of these, in turn, to refine the vision. Continue to ask 'why' for each statement until there are a set of 'outcome' vision statements. They differ from 'milestone' statements in the following ways:

- They are within your ability to influence.
- They can never be finished – no matter how much time you spend with your kids today, they will still want to spend time with you tomorrow.

- They can be achieved continuously – while you can't earn a college degree in a day, you can learn something new in a moment.

Your new perspective may look something like this:

- Improve my family's financial security
- Develop my relationships with my family and close friends
- Do meaningful work, in an ethical way, that helps others
- Support charitable causes that align with my values
- Continually learn and grow

This is a personal vision that is compelling and expansive. It reduces the chance of achieving milestones, at the expense of the outcomes truly desired.

Step 2: Form a Position

A position is the stance taken by an organization to achieve its perspective – its unique value proposition. This idea also applies to career choices. We do this without even realizing it. Newer supervisors emphasize their energy, willingness to work long hours, and cutting-edge ideas. Experienced managers market their work accomplishments, network of resources, and knowledge of industries and firms.

There are many potential pitfalls in forming a position:

- Narrowly defining capabilities – experiences in one industry, or situation, are more transferable than commonly recognized.
- Falsely representing abilities – not only is it wrong, it is far too easily identified in today's connected world.
- Ineffectively communicating value proposition – employers and clients are far too busy to read between the lines.

The worst error you can make is all too common. *Don't form a position that conflicts with your perspective.* Say you want to have a great relationship with your children. Offering to travel anywhere, anytime, at a moment's notice, would be a mistake. You would end up canceling planned events, missing important events, and undermining your relationship. This misalignment leads to a terrible outcome – accomplishments that do not provide meaningful value.

Regardless of the position you want to have, you must know your actual position too. Professionals often do not understand how they appear to others. Employers and clients can only give credit for what they can see, hear and experience. For example, you may apply for a position and have many relevant accomplishments, while a competitor has few. If you both only list your prior responsibilities on your resumes, how will the hiring manager distinguish between you in a resume screening? Hint: they won't!

Stakeholders can provide valuable input on each element of their personal vision and position. For example, criteria to evaluate in the professional space could include the following items:

- Reputation and brand in their network
- Value shown in resumes and cover letters
- Performance in interviews, presentations, and other persuasive situations
- Awareness and credibility by key industries and organizations
- Capabilities and skills in comparison to potential competitors

You will most likely find that the outside view differs from your desired internal view and your previously defined perspective. You may be discouraged. Don't be! You now have the key ingredients to create strategic plans.

Step 3: Craft and execute Plans

'Strategy, as a plan, is a course of action from one point to another within a competitive scenario.' ITIL v3 Service Strategy

Enterprises use strategic plans to improve their strategic positioning. For example, a firm that serves government agencies wants to increase market share. Its research determines an unmet need for a new product. The strategic plan oversees development of the new product. The firm's completion of the plan results in an improved position.

Your strategic plan has the same intent. Fortunately, you've already done the hard parts! Your perspective provides the criteria for success. Your position provides the current state for each criterion. The plan is simply a high-level approach to move from your current position, to a new position more in line with your perspective.

There are only a few steps required to develop your strategic plan:

1. For each item in the perspective, identify your new desired state. If you want to support charitable causes, you may set a target of at least two hours of volunteer work per month.
2. Create a list of ideas on how to achieve the combined set of items. Consider ways to achieve multiple items through a single action (e.g. volunteering at your child's school, or activity, can build relationships, contribute to the community, and develop new skills).
3. Select the best group of ideas aligned to the perspective.

Your result? A personal strategic plan focused on value, based in reality, and biased for action. Consider it your personal charter for success!

Step 4: Adopt Patterns of action

Strategic plans only create value when we put them into action. They create guardrails for design, enable focus during transition, provide guidance in operation, and form the basis for improvement. Processes, references, and decision criteria, are a few types of action patterns. The result is capabilities used to deliver services.

Each of these stages also provides input back into the strategy. Intentional actions always have unintended consequences. Employee actions to reduce returned product significantly affect brand reputation. A minor investment in online advertising becomes a big success. Hiring guidance attracts a culture of workaholics.

Unintended consequences also occur in your personal strategy. You must be flexible to exploit opportunities and minimize drawbacks. Yet actions also form patterns, such as credibility, integrity and reliability. If you deliver, on time, with high quality, you will earn a reputation for delivering value – and more opportunities to do so. Negative patterns reduce the odds of success. How, then, can you be nimble as things change? By using a simple approach to maintain an effective strategy:

1. Put your strategy into action.
2. Regularly review your results through observation and measurement.

3. Feed this information back into the start of your strategic lifecycle.

The lifecycle approach to strategy balances stability and agility. This balance provides the foundation for your personal success. A foundation by itself, though, is of little value. You must build on it! *Chapter 2* will outline how to apply good design principles to begin putting your strategy into action.

Action plan

- Identify your statements of success. Use the 5 Whys tool to turn milestone statements into outcome statements.
- Determine your current position. Ask peers, friends, family, etc. for candid input.
- Create a plan to improve your current state. Look for ideas that help you in more than one area.
- Execute, review results, and refine.

CHAPTER 2: USING DESIGN COORDINATION FOR YOUR PERSONAL SERVICES

'Systems thinking shows there is no outside; that you and the cause of your problems are part of a single system.'
– Peter Senge

Most people do not plan for success, and it shows. They focus on the unimportant. They spend on the unnecessary. They deliver on the useless.

ITIL defines a system as 'a series of related things that work together to achieve an objective.' Thus, we can call how you deliver results your 'personal effectiveness system' (PES). Your PES has a design, even if unplanned. The good news is that ITSM thinking can help you whip your PES into shape!

ITIL identifies five elements of a holistic design. They are the service solutions, service management systems and tools, architectures, measurements, and processes. Let's apply this framework to your PES.

Element 1: Design the service solutions you will deliver

A service solution is the mix of goods and services that meet a need. ITIL states that services are composed of resources and capabilities. This leads to our first rule: *don't define a service solution you can't deliver*. The best way to avoid this pitfall is to identify your capabilities and resources first.

Capabilities

- Management – There's that word again! In this context, management refers to the classic ability to 'do things right.'
  - o Can you execute to a plan?
  - o Can you get others to do so?
- Organization – This typically refers to hierarchies and reporting structures. Think of this as your ability to apply your resources to create value.
  - o What assistance (real and virtual) can you call on to perform tasks?

- o How 'in the loop' are you when others do things on your behalf?
- Processes – We will discuss processes later on in *Chapter 2*. For now, consider your ability to define how you work.
  - o Can you describe what you do in a few key steps?
  - o Do you know who your customers are, and how they define quality?
- Knowledge – We will discuss knowledge management in depth in *Chapter 3*. For this situation, focus on your current state of knowledge.
  - o What models, frameworks, and approaches are you certified in, familiar with, and/or able to apply?
  - o How well can you learn and grow?

Resources

- Financial capital – Money can cover up many gaps. Lack of money limits options.
  - o How much money could you access to take advantage of a 'golden opportunity'?
  - o What existing commitments restrict your freedom?
- Infrastructure – Our equipment affects how we work. Consider how laptops changed workplaces in the early 2000s.
  - o How do your existing devices enable, or restrict, the kinds of tasks you can perform?
  - o What limits do you face when you are away from your home and work spaces?
- Applications – Applications enable us to perform useful tasks. They greatly affect our efficiency and effectiveness.
  - o What applications can you access?
  - o How well can you use them to get work done?
- Information – Access to the right information is a critical success factor.
  - o What information sources do you use?
  - o How often does new information change how you approach your work?

Use the resources and capabilities you have to define the services you will offer. How to do this? Engage the most important resource and capability: you! Your work ethic, creativity, and insight are just a few of the attributes you bring to the table.

- Identify the unmet needs you see in everyday life, social media, and job postings.
- Review your resources and capabilities that could help meet those needs. Don't forget the services and systems that others provide you.
- Define your service solutions based on the need you will meet, and the resources and capabilities you will use.

Element 2: Design the service management systems and tools you will use to manage your services

A core principle of ITIL is to manage things that matter throughout their lifecycle. The services we defined in Part 1 are no different. The primary ITSM system and tool recommended by ITIL for this purpose is the service portfolio. While we will discuss service portfolio management in depth in *Chapter 11*, we must consider a few key items now for our PES.

- Create a list of your defined services and their attributes.
  - o What do your customers get from the service?
  - o What resources and capabilities are required to deliver the service?
- Identify the lifecycle stage for each service.
  - o Which services are you delivering and actively provide value?
  - o Which services are you building and testing?
  - o Which services are still in the idea stage?

The service portfolio provides a single view into how you provide value. Here are just a few ways it can help you.

- Find opportunities for new services with your existing customers.
- Identify services that overlap or conflict.
- See what services warrant further investment – and those that should be retired.

Element 3: Design the architectures for your services

Many people in IT say they want to be in architecture. For many, it is because they view it as a high-paying job that can't be outsourced, that tells other people what to do. Sounds great, right? But ask those people what architects *actually do* and you will rarely hear the same answer twice. Even authorities disagree on what architecture means in IT.

ITIL defines architecture as 'the structure of a system or IT service,' as well as the relationships, standards, and guidelines of the structure. Since your PES is a system, you are an architect! Just consider the subsystems that make up your PES:

- Communication systems
- Productivity systems
- Mobility systems
- Connectivity systems
- Computing systems
- Creativity and presentation systems
- Knowledge management systems (gathering, storage, retention, analysis)
- Transportation systems
- Personal well-being systems (health, finance, spiritual)
- Relationship management systems (family, service providers, regulatory)
- Acquisition systems
- Improvement systems
- Entertainment systems
- Specialized systems for your unique service offerings

That's quite a list! Notice a couple of things about this list.

- None of these systems is new, just the technologies. For example, computing systems include finger counting, abacuses, and long division.
- Multiple systems can use the same resources and capabilities. A horse can be a resource for both a transportation system and an entertainment system.

We have filled our world with poorly designed business and personal architectures. They have redundant tools that don't work well together. They are time-consuming to maintain and upgrade. To make things worse, they are resistant to change when something better comes along. When you spend more time updating your applications than you spend using them, poor architecture is why!

So how can you make your PES easier to maintain, and cheaper? Here is one approach based on good enterprise architecture practices:

- Identify the resources and capabilities you use for each system.
- For each item, determine what other systems it could also support. For instance, a magazine subscription could be a part of entertainment and personal health systems.
- Focus on your unitaskers – those items that only support one system. Does it provide unique value? Could another resource, or capability, do the job competently? If so, get rid of it!
- Look at systems where you have a lot of resources and capabilities. Are you using multiple tools to do the same thing? Could you get 95% of the value from just one or two items? Don't use 12 tools where three will do just as well!
- Review the resources and capabilities that support many systems. What can they do that you are not using? Is there a core set of items that would cover most, or all, of your needs?
- Maximize the value of your 'core architecture.' For example, there may be a way to integrate two systems so they work well together. This is a worthy investment for core items.

The ideal state is to use a few resources and capabilities to their limits, and supplement them where there are gaps or unique value. Even a five-ten percent reduction in money and time spent will pay off in the end!

Element 4: Design the measurements and metrics for your services

'Measure twice, cut once.' Anyone who has ever built a house knows the importance of measurement. The same is true of your life. Have you ever spent time on a task, only to realize at the end that you have no idea if what you did actually made things better? Poor metrics are usually to blame. This is a core focus of ITIL and this book. Measurement is the foundation of improvement.

At this point, it is essential to know what success looks like before taking action. There is a secret to doing this well. *Define your measures of success from your customer's perspective.* As ITIL repeatedly states, the customer ultimately determines value. They do not care how many hours you spent developing your service, or how hard it was to deliver. Their concern is getting sufficient value from your service for the money, time, and energy they spend.

Another mistake is using only objective measures to determine value. Yes, you need objective measures. Don't forget, though, that value is a subjective experience. There is no substitute for asking your customers what value they received from your service. While there are many tools, such as SERVQUAL, that do this very well, you don't need anything complex to get started. Here is a simple approach based on a concept called Net Promoter Score:

- Ask the people who depend on your work if they would recommend your services to others. Include your peers, your boss, and anyone else that receives your work products.
- Classify each person, based on their feedback, into three buckets: those that would recommend your work to others, those who would discourage others from using your work, and those that do not feel strongly either way.
- Count the number of people that would recommend your work. Subtract the count of people who would discourage others. Divide this number by the total number of people you asked for feedback.
  o If this value is negative, fix the flaws that cause the negative view of your results.
  o If it's between 0% and 20%, it is likely you are not getting candid feedback. The cure for this is improving relationships, which is a major focus in Part II of this book.
  o If it is greater than 20%, ask your advocates why they would recommend your services. Strive to deliver that value to everyone you support.

The hardest part of measurement is getting started. Don't wait until you can produce 'true' metrics. That day will never come! Put something in place, even if it is flawed.

Element 5: Design the processes that support your services

ITIL has a lot to say about processes. It defines them as '*a structured set of activities designed to accomplish a specific objective.*' This is a turnoff to many folks. What comes to mind when you see the word 'process': long lines? Endless forms? Eternal waits? Smug paper-pushers? Scary!

So why don't we just avoid processes altogether? The fact is, we cannot. At the most basic level, a process describes how to change something into something else. For example, here is a process description of a meal:

- Obtain food
- Prepare food
- Serve food
- Eat food

It is impossible to have a meal without performing these steps. Does this mean your next lunch will require a ten-page form and an hour's wait? No! Those sorts of things depend on goals, resources, and capabilities outside the process.

We have established that we cannot avoid processes. How can we design them for effective use? You may have heard of Six Sigma. It is a set of tools and techniques for process improvement. SIPOC is a popular Six Sigma tool that guides process design by considering Suppliers, Inputs, Process, Outputs, and Customers. Here is a useful way to apply this tool to designing your services:

- Identify the customers of your service. Who will primarily use the outputs, or be affected by them? For our meal, this would be the diners eating the meal.
- Determine the outputs the customers primarily want from the service. Our diners may want a cheap and tasty meal. Perhaps they would prefer a healthful and filling meal. Maybe they desire a romantic and fun experience.
- Define the process to deliver the outputs. Our four-step process from above will work fine for now. Resist the urge to call out more than five steps at this time.
- Call out the inputs needed by the process to produce the desired outputs. Some of our meal inputs could include prepared foods, ingredients, cookware, dishes, and recipes.
- Select the suppliers that will provide the inputs. Our meal inputs could come from grocery stores, cookbooks, or the local pizza place.

Doing this work will help you focus on what matters. It can also identify areas where automation can help, or where it is more trouble than it is worth. One more benefit is that a documented process is easier to measure.

These five elements feed into each other. Your process designs, for instance, will help define your measurements. The important thing is to account for all of these areas. They will be refined as we progress through the lifecycle.

Now you have your value stream – a clearly defined set of services, and the elements needed to build them. In the next two chapters, we will use ITSM thinking to help you set up two critical systems – knowledge management systems (*Chapter 3*) and communication systems (*Chapter 4*).

Action plan

- Design your Personal Effectiveness System (PES)
    o Define your services based on your resources and capabilities
    o Document the key attributes of your services to create your service portfolio
    o Review the tools in your PES and improve these using good architectural practices
    o Write down your measures of success from your customer's point of view
    o Use SIPOC to create your processes
- Review your PES against your statements of success from *Chapter 1*. Are they aligned? If not, document the gaps for improvement

CHAPTER 3: BUILDING YOUR SERVICE KNOWLEDGE MANAGEMENT SYSTEM

'A manager is responsible for the application and performance of knowledge.' – Peter Drucker

Do you struggle to decide what to eat for lunch? If so, I have some bad news. **Decision making is the most valuable thing managers do.** Decisions drive outcomes. A good decision enables us to exploit opportunities and minimize risks. But fear not! The ability to make good decisions is a skill you can learn.

Many people (including managers) will tell you that there is no shortcut to improved decision making. They say that it can only come from experience as a manager. These people are wrong! Even if you're not a manager (yet), you can build this skill. How? By applying knowledge management thinking to the decision process.

Chapter 2 mentioned knowledge management systems as one element of your PES. ITIL refers to this as a Service Knowledge Management System (SKMS). It defines knowledge management as 'the process responsible for sharing perspectives, ideas, experience and information, and for ensuring that these are available in the right place and at the right time.' Think of it as how to store your experiences and insights in your personal SKMS.

To improve your decision-making ability, you must become good at two things: filling your SKMS, and using your SKMS. How do you do this? Use what ITIL refers to as the 'Data-to-Information-to-Knowledge-to-Wisdom structure,' or 'DIKW.' Here is how to use DIKW as a decision-making approach.

Step 1: Collect good data

Data are facts about experiences and insights. A scribbled idea is a data element. So is your bank account balance. Our world is awash in data but it vanishes as quickly as it appears if we do not capture it. Here are some techniques for increasing the amount of data you capture:

- Record your ideas as they occur. Carry a pad and paper at all times. Keep writing materials near your bed, for when inspiration strikes at midnight. Call your phone when you have an idea and leave a message. Use mobile devices to capture notes or voice recordings. Send yourself an email or text. Read with a highlighter.

- Use automated systems. Quantified Self (QS) devices can capture vast amounts of personal data. Macros and scripts can be set up to record data about how often you use email and social media. Use online clipping services, e-readers, and data feeds, to provide input to trigger ideas and flag data sources for future use.

- Set aside time to have ideas. This may be while you meditate, mow the lawn, or exercise. Just make sure to record them when they happen!

- Interact with a wide variety of people. The more diversity in your social circles, the more you will be exposed to other ways of thinking. The experiences and insights of others are valuable – capture them!

Step 2: Use the right data for the decision

You may be familiar with the expression 'garbage in, garbage out.' How do we identify, and avoid, garbage data? Here are some good data rules to follow:

- Use data relevant to the goal or objective. While this sounds obvious, it is easy to rely on the same data sets over and over again. For example, a technician may be measured on how many incidents she fixes per day. If she is promoted to manager, is this still a relevant measure of her performance? No!

- Don't overwhelm yourself with data. Modern systems can provide a data avalanche with the push of a button. You will rarely benefit from huge data sets. Limit data to a manageable portion. You can always get more data later if you need it.

- Understand the data source(s). Obtaining data is often easier than comprehending it. You should be able to answer these questions about the data:
  o What triggers creation of data? Is it created at defined intervals, or when certain conditions occur?

o What does each data field mean? If it is a numeric value, what units do the numbers represent?

o Are there multiple systems, or people, recording the data? If so, examine a sample from each input source to ensure consistency.

o What incentives are there for the data to be right? What data quality checks are performed on the data? How are data changes controlled? If the answer is 'none,' be cautious in using the data.

• Use timely data. The value of data declines the more things change. In stable areas, data from years ago can be usable. In chaotic situations, data from yesterday may be garbage.

Step 3: Process the data into information

ITIL refers to information as data that has been put into context. Databases, spreadsheet tables and such, are already structured. Data collected manually in tables and grids needs little work as well. So why do we call this out as a separate step? Because there is a whole set of data that needs attention – your ideas and insights!

Most people miss this entirely. The result is that they don't apply all they know to decisions. Simply entering your scribblings into a list is a start. However, it does not provide context. You need something more effective for your data. Fortunately, you can use several approaches to provide structure:

• Create idea categories and file each insight under the most relevant entry. This requires the least upfront work. It works best for thoughts that are specific to a technology, or body of knowledge.

• Use tagging systems and flag ideas by relevant concepts. This often provides more value than filing, yet requires more work per entry. It allows for multiple contexts of your thoughts.

• Use mind maps to show the relationships between thoughts. This is the most powerful approach, as it provides the most context. It also requires the most effort to learn how to use it effectively.

Your data has been processed when you can look at it and identify patterns. The data may vary by location, time, people, technology, and other factors. Learning to do this well can improve your decision quality dramatically!

Step 4: Analyze the information to glean knowledge

Analysis is best defined as breaking down, and interpreting, information. This step is where we transition from filling our personal SKMS, to using it. Keep the following thoughts in mind when doing analysis:

- Analysis is more than just identifying trends. You must dig deeper into underlying factors. One way to do this is by using the '5 Whys' tool we discussed in *Chapter 1*.

- Question your assumptions. Consider your bank account going up. Is that good? Most people would agree without thinking. What if it's because none of your bills are getting paid? It's easy to jump to the most favorable answer when we see a trend. It's also often wrong.

- Don't jump to conclusions. Like all other people, you are great at seeing patterns – even when they do not exist. Is this problem truly just like one you have used before? Take another look and make sure.

- Use the right tool for the job. Do you always use pie charts to graph information? While this is great for comparing categories, it's terrible for time-based information. Don't use a screwdriver to do a hammer's job!

- Review your ruts. Are you asking the same three people for their opinions on any trend you see? You may be missing valuable input.

Notice a theme? The biggest fault most people have with analysis is that they don't do any! At this time, analysis can rarely be done by computers. It requires your time and your attention. If you are not thinking, no one is! This is another area where a little effort can produce large benefits.

Step 5: Use your knowledge to make the best decision

Once you have completed your analysis, it is time to create wisdom. In this context, wisdom is making the best decision, given your circumstances. Most people equate decisions with choices. They are not quite the same thing. Drucker corrects this common view by defining a decision as a choice and a set of actions. Choices, by themselves, do not produce value, only actions can!

While there are many ways to approach developing a recommendation, here is a simple approach that you can refine as you go. Let's use an example of wanting to improve your health.

- Write down a clear problem statement about your situation. Be specific. The statement should relate to your goals. Don't just write down 'I want to get healthier.' A statement like 'In order to be around to watch my kids grow up, I want to reduce my body fat by five percent in the next six months,' is much closer to the mark.

- Determine the criteria to use for evaluating your options. A good guideline is to aim for five to ten factors. For our example we will use cost, likelihood of reaching our target, expected enjoyment level, time required, amount of support from family/friends, and sustainability.

- Start generating options. Review your SKMS with your problem statement in mind. You will find that ideas will occur to you. Write them down, even if they are terrible. Aim for at least 20 options. If you are stuck on less than ten, you either need to stop filtering your ideas, or go find more data sources. With practice, you will be able to do this in less than 15 minutes.

- Eliminate the worst options from your list. Some of your ideas will be clearly inferior to others. Cross them out. As you do so, identify any kernels of value that may need to be accounted for in your action plan. Document them for later.

- Create a cross-hatch grid. In the left-most column, list each of your criteria. At the top of each column, list each option still being considered. Don't forget to add 'status quo' as an option. There is always an option to do nothing. Including it accomplishes two important things:
  1. It reduces the chances that you won't make a decision at all. This is the same as choosing the status quo, which can be a terrible outcome. Explicitly including it as an option reduces the chances you will choose it by default.
  2. Sometimes the status quo is the best option. You don't want to leave your best choice out of your consideration.

- Populate the grid. Don't worry about being precise. High/Medium/Low or a one to five scale is more than adequate. If you want to explain your score, do so in the box. *Table 1* is a sample for our health goal.

Table 1: Decision criteria

	Status quo	Join a gym	Join Weight Watchers	Fad diet
Cost	Low	High	Medium	Low
Likelihood of reaching target	Low	High	High	Medium
Expected enjoyment level	Medium	Low	Medium	Low
Time required	Low	High	Medium	Medium
Amount of support	Medium	Low (don't know anyone there)	High (spouse is a member)	Low
Sustainability	High	Medium	Medium	Low

- Pick the best option. Often you will find that the best choice is obvious because you have applied your knowledge well. Other times, you may struggle to choose from two or three options – the dreaded 'analysis paralysis.' Some people will propose weighting your criteria and mathematically determining the best choice. That may be helpful, yet in most cases choosing weighting values, and such, actually makes for worse choices. Try these things instead, to break the impasse.
  o Try to combine elements of your options. Often you can create a better option that will become the obvious choice.
  o Start to create an action plan for each option. You will often find that one action plan comes much easier, or the actions from one option can be applied to another, to create a clearly best decision.
  o Discuss the dilemma with someone you trust. You will often get additional insights that can tip the scales.
  o If you're still stuck, flip a coin, or just pick an option and execute it as well as you can. If the decision is that close, it is best to just choose and move on.
- Develop the action plan for your option (if you have not done so already). Make sure each element of the plan has three things: an owner, a specific activity, and a deadline.
- Get started!

Step 6: Review your decisions regularly

Knowledge management has a lifecycle just like everything else. To close the loop, review your decision 60-90 days after it was made.

Ask yourself the following questions, note them in your SKMS, and make adjustments to your decision process as appropriate.

- How well did I execute the action plan? Can I truly tell if I made the right choice or not?
- Are there criteria that I should have included?
- Was my decision relevant to my goals, or did I drift during my decision process?
- Was my analysis of root causes accurate, or was it too shallow?
- Were my analysis tools the right ones to use?
- Are there errors in my data, or information, that are now apparent? What steps can I take to check for them next time?
- Did I apply my insights and experiences well? Did I miss relevant info because of poor classification?
- What did I learn?
- What worked well?

The final advice for improving decision making is to practice. Use this approach on your personal decisions. When helping your bosses and others, identify your role in their decisions and practice those skills. Even if you're just gathering data for others, you can still improve and provide value.

While there are no shortcuts to becoming a great decision maker, you can still improve rapidly compared to most people. They will repeat the same mistakes over and over. Even just making every mistake once is far better!

Another key skill for future managers is being able to manage your work efficiently and effectively. In *Chapter 4* we will examine how good use of event management principles can improve your communication system.

Action plan

- Create your personal SKMS
  - o Define methods to capture your experiences and insights
  - o Create a structure for storing your ideas, so they can be accessed when needed

- Practice making decisions using the process described
  - o Set aside time to do analysis
  - o Create recommendations based on the analysis
- Regularly review your knowledge practices for areas of improvement

CHAPTER 4: SIMPLIFY YOUR COMMUNICATIONS WITH EVENT MANAGEMENT

'That's been one of my mantras – focus and simplicity. Simple can be harder than complex: You have to work hard to get your thinking clean to make it simple. But it's worth it in the end because once you get there, you can move mountains.' – Steve Jobs

Are you a slave to your communications system? Do you allow your computer and/or phone to constantly interrupt you? Would someone observing you for a week think your job was to check your messages? This is a common situation and is horribly ineffective.

The specific tools – email, IM, texts, RSS feeds, social media, etc., have changed, and will continue to change. What stays the same? The need to manage them to meet your needs. It's time to take control!

Let's talk about value. You designed your value stream in *Chapter 2*. Lean thinking tells us that your value stream consists of three types of activities:

1. Activities that create value
2. Activities that don't create value and can be avoided
3. Activities that don't create value yet seem unavoidable

Most of your activities with your communications system fall into the last category. Reading your email, for example, may be necessary. It does not create value on its own. Thus, the goals of your communications system are as follows:

- Minimize the time spent managing communications
- Identify tasks and ideas to improve provided value
- Maintain relationships with customers and your network

How can ITSM thinking help you do these things?

ITIL's event management process is ideally suited to your needs. That may sound strange to you. We often associate this process with giant monitors and flashing lights. What does that have to do with texts and instant messages?

Your computer can produce more messages in a minute than you could read in the rest of your life. Which messages are valuable? Recall our discussion of data in *Chapter 3*. You need a reasonable amount of relevant data. Therefore, you only want to see messages that indicate an exception. A disk is failing. An update installed. You have a task that needs to be done by the end of the week.

Event management, at its core, is about identifying exceptions in a sea of data. Let's explore how the event management process can help you manage your communications system.

Step 1: Define your communications system architecture

List each way you receive communications from others. Count every physical and virtual inbox, phone number, and social system. Don't forget about in-person channels, such as conversations and meetings. You should also include anything that you use to obtain news and opinions, such as blogs.

Simplify your communications system architecture. Use the ideas in *Chapter 2* to improve your PES. Combine multiple inboxes. Eliminate redundant tools. Use services that effectively manage multiple tools.

Step 2: For each tool, define how to handle the three types of communications

Just like event monitoring tools, you must define effective rules to be successful. The challenge is doing this when the tools we use seem to change constantly. Good news! Regardless of what happens with technology, communications can be classified into three main types, see *table 2*:

Table 2: Communication types

Type	Response expected?	Action expected?	Intended audience	Examples
Streams	No	No	Public	Town crier, newspapers, TV news, press events, blogs, spam, telemarketing, webinars, Twitter
Announcements	No	Yes	Group	Edicts, judgments, org-wide e-mails, all-hands meetings, conference sessions
Discussions	Yes	Yes	You + Possibly others	Meetings, phone calls, instant messaging, conversations, self-service systems

Don't mistake one type for another. You either waste time and energy by over reacting, or get negative consequences from under reacting. Most tools allow all three types. For example, email presents spam, organizational announcements, and conversations, all mixed together. Treating each of these the same way will lead to disaster.

The solution is simple. For each tool you use, decide how you will handle each communication type:

• Streams provide a constant influx of data. Focus on filtering. Eliminate sources that are high noise and low signal. Find ways to quickly identify useful data and get rid of the rest. Useful data goes into your personal SKMS (see Chapter 3). Don't try to keep up or catch up. There will be another batch of news in ten minutes anyway.

• Announcements are less frequent yet more tailored. Focus on translation. You must turn general guidance into specific actions you will take. Schedule tasks in your productivity system and follow through. Update your SKMS, as needed, for future reference.

• Discussions are the most specific and require the most care. Every discussion impacts two things – the topic of discussion, and the relationship between participants. Both parts are important. Focus on the discussion. Do not try to multitask when responding. Set rules around each tool to guide how often you check for messages, how quickly you must respond, when to escalate to other communication methods, and how formal to make your messages.

One common pitfall is that we tend to either respond more quickly than truly needed, or not at all when we should. This is particularly true of email. You DO NOT need to respond to emails instantly, unless your job is providing email support to external customers. Millions of professionals that receive more email than you will only spend three 30-minute sessions in email today. For help with this, check out *Getting Things Done* by David Allen.

Step 3: Run your communication system following your guidelines

How well would an event system work if it only alerted you *sometimes* when a threshold was hit? The same is true for your communication system. It's easy to just pull up your email or IM when you should be doing something useful. This causes two issues:

1. You've substituted a non-value-creating activity for a value-creating activity.
2. You are varying your event thresholds.

Neither of these things are good in the long run! Give it a good faith effort for at least a week. Treat it as an experiment, a fact-finding mission. Here are some other tips to help you be successful:

- Only handle each communication once. Remove it from your communication system once handled. Unnecessary motion, such as reopening messages, is wasteful.
- Keep your communication and productivity activities separated. You can use the same tool for both. Just be clear when your communications have transitioned to tasks or data.
- Use richer communication channels, such as face-to-face or video chat, for more complex messages. This reduces misinterpretation. It is also more efficient, in most cases, compared to text-based messaging.
- Be brief and clear.

Step 4: Review and adjust your thresholds regularly

After at least a week, review how well your communication system is working. Use these questions to assess how things are going:

- How much time did you spend managing your communications system?
- How many new ideas did you get from your streams?
- Did you meet your targets for response to discussions?
- Did any announcements or discussions get missed by your system?
- Were there any low-value patterns in your streams that need to be filtered going forward?

Make adjustments, as needed, to make your system more effective and efficient. Remember – your communications system should help you achieve your statements of success. Don't let it become your master!

Action plan

- Identify all of your communications tools
- Determine how to identify and handle your feeds, announcements, and discussions, in each communication tool
- Set up weekly reviews of your system, and make changes to minimize time managing the system while maintaining quality

CHAPTER 5: APPLYING CONTINUAL SERVICE IMPROVEMENT TO YOUR LEARNING

'Adapt or perish, now as ever, is Nature's inexorable imperative.' – H.G. Wells

Everything decays. Relationships wither. Customers go. New systems stagnate. Hot skills cool.

What can you count on? Your ability to learn, change, and grow. The essential skill of our age is to continually improve. This does not mean spending hours learning how to brush your teeth faster. The point is to use the limited time and resources you have to increase your value to yourself and others.

The bad news is that many improvement efforts fail. Why? Fear. You may be afraid of failure, embarrassment, being out of the loop, looking dumb, losing face, appearing foolish, and even of success! You need an approach that can help you overcome your fear. Call it improving your ability to improve!

This need is addressed by ITIL in the Continual Service Improvement (CSI) lifecycle stage. You may be familiar with other approaches, such as the scientific method, PDCA, DMAIC and Kaizen. They all have a similar root. You do not improve with the goal of reaching a permanent stable state. There is no such thing! Like a tree that bends towards sunlight and sways with the wind, your permanent state is one of adjusting and improving.

You've already seen CSI in action. The earlier discussions of the four Ps of strategy, your PES, your personal SKMS, and your communications system, included a review and adjustment stage. It will continue to be a theme throughout this book.

This approach can be applied to **anything**. Becoming happier. Getting a raise. Losing weight. Starting a business. Growing more spiritual. Finding a mate. Anything! Here is how to use the CSI model for learning.

Step 1: What is your vision?

Refer back to your statements of success from *Chapter 1*. Did you have a statement about learning and growth? If not, you should add one! This is not about getting a Harvard MBA, an ITIL Expert certification, or any other milestone. Instead, it is about challenging yourself, doing your best, and learning every day.

The best way to do this is to adopt the mindset of being open and honest about what you don't know. Practice this phrase regularly: 'I don't know.' Go ahead, try it out loud right now. Learning starts with an admission of ignorance. We are conditioned to fake being 'in the know' out of fear. Don't be afraid to learn!

Step 2: Where are you now?

How open are you to learning and growth? You probably have a vague answer. That is why baselining your current state is important. It's not complex – answering these questions will give you a starting point:

- How often do you look up things you encounter that you don't know?
- What was the last voluntary training session you attended?
- When was the last time someone asked you something you didn't know and you answered 'I don't know'?
- When did you last obtain a certification or degree?
- What was the last task you volunteered for that you had not done before?
- Do you remember the last person you asked for help with a problem you were facing?

As you practice, you will come up with your own questions to add to this list. The key is to document how things are right now. Beware the 'curse of knowledge.' Once your state of mind changes, it's impossible to remember what it was like. If you don't capture it now, you won't be able to tell how much progress you make later!

Step 3: Where do you want to be?

This is the step where milestones become useful. Your vision is not a goal to be reached. It is a navigation aid, like the North Star. You now want to create your target. Here is a powerful technique to help you create your target state:

- Identify the pain points in your life from not learning and growing. Are you missing out on exciting assignments? Did you not get the promotion you wanted? Are you facing the same kinds of problems over and over? Be specific.

- Pick one of them. Most people make the mistake of trying to fix too many pain points at once. Don't mistake limiting your focus now with making permanent choices.

- Determine how you will know when the pain point has been fixed. This may be simple, such as achieving a certification. Others may require more thought. For example, you may want to improve your ability to do research. A simple measure may be to mark your calendar each day you use a reference to answer a question. Don't make this too hard. A yes/no measure is ideal for starting out.

- Write your target state down, and post it where you will see it every morning. This will remind you of your target and get you to think about achieving it.

Step 4: How do you get there?

You are now ready to create your action plan. Poor plans are usually caused by a few issues. The tasks are broad and unclear. The deadlines are loose – or not stated at all. They don't separate what you can control and what you need from others. Try this lifecycle approach to planning instead.

- Identify the first few things to be done. Do not try to plan the whole improvement at once. You will either give up trying to create the plan, or you will become too rigid in executing.

- Estimate the time required to perform each task. If any of them will take more than 90 minutes of your effort, create smaller sub tasks. The mind rapidly loses focuses after 90 minutes. Work within this limit and you will be more likely to complete tasks. For instance, 'read book' is too broad. Specify a chapter, or even just part of a chapter.

- Review each task for dependencies on others. Make sub tasks for any portions you cannot perform yourself. Specify who must perform the task, how you will engage them, and how you will follow up. This helps you manage these items more effectively, without interrupting what you can accomplish on your own.

- Schedule enough time on your calendar for task work. Your calendar is not just a meeting receptacle! It helps you manage your priorities. Experiment with generic calendar time for tasks and scheduling specific tasks. Use the approach that gets you the best results.

Step 5: Did you get there?

Reviewing progress regularly makes all the difference. Schedule a weekly check-up on your improvement.

- Look for successful patterns and reuse them. What scheduled activities did you stick to? Are certain times of day particularly good for getting tasks done? What follow-up techniques work best for your dependencies?
- Assess where you fell short and why. Are certain task types chronic issues? Is there a 'stuck' dependency? Do you allow certain types of distractions to interrupt your focus?
- Review the tasks not done. Do they still need to be done? Should they be further broken down? What can you change to get them completed?
- Identify the next batch of tasks using the rules in Step 4 and schedule them.

Step 6: How do you keep the momentum going?

An important point about improvement **– shorter review cycles are better.** A bus driver makes constant adjustments to the steering wheel to stay on the road. If she only adjusted every ten seconds, the bus would violently swerve, until it ended up in a ditch.

Most improvement projects end up 'in the ditch' for the same reason. Monthly task reviews don't work. You can easily lose three weeks you would have saved from a weekly review. Over time, that adds up to delays and lost momentum.

Don't forget to celebrate your successes. Since we are focused on learning to improve, there are many types of progress:

- Tasks completed
- What you learned from trying to do the improvement
- Patterns you identified that help or hinder success

- Less time and energy required to do planning
- More scheduled time focused on tasks and avoiding distractions

---

You now have a holistic approach to your success and growth.

- Define success and a strategy to achieve it
- Design your services to get the outcomes you want
- Transition data into usable knowledge
- Operate an effective communication system
- Continually improve your ability to learn

In Part II, we will examine how to improve managing your team. How can you balance their needs with enterprise goals? Service management thinking offers many tools that can help!

Action plan

- Add a learning and growth entry to your statements of success
- Regularly assess, and improve, your ability to adjust and learn
- Commit to self-development as a way of life, not something to finish

PART II: EFFECTIVENESS WITH YOUR TEAM

'You cannot continuously improve interdependent systems and processes until you progressively perfect interdependent, interpersonal relationships.' – Stephen Covey

Relationships matter. Being the smartest person in the room is a dead-end. Power is no longer about threats and bluster. What works? Understanding and connecting. Your ability to work through others is no longer optional.

CHAPTER 6: USING BUSINESS RELATIONSHIP MANAGEMENT THINKING TO FORM A GREAT TEAM

'The secret to success is good leadership, and good leadership is all about making the lives of your team members or workers better.' – Tony Dungy

Most managers are not worthy of the title. They undermine their staff. They lurch from crisis to crisis. They hog the credit and share the blame. They are vague and smarmy. The result? Missed deadlines. Angry customers. Lost superstars. Depressing!

How can you avoid joining this club? The good news is that good management is simple. *Hire great people and develop them to be successful.* The bad news is that it is not easy! Mike Auzenne and Mark Horstman of *Manager Tools* say it best – 'success is about results and relationships.'

ITIL defines a relationship as 'a connection or interaction between two people or things.' ITIL 2011 edition describes business relationship management as essential for delivering value. Your direct reports expect value from their work. Money is the obvious one, yet there are also drivers, such as respect, purpose, and a sense of contribution to a greater good.

You may think that a manager-direct report relationship is different because of power. Good luck telling your customers what to do! But power is really just another form of relationship. A manager only has three types of power at their disposal. These roughly align with Aristotle's three modes of persuasion:

1. Ethos is the 'appeal to authority.' This roughly aligns with your role power. Your organization gives you a certain amount of rewards and punishments you can use to influence behaviors. Bad managers overuse this. The result is a compliance culture where people only do what is required and no more. This is a losing strategy! The less you use your role power, the more effective it is when you **do** use it.

2. Logos is the 'appeal to logic.' Consider this your power from your expertise. You may be able to persuade others due to your knowledge of a tool, a process, or a technique. This is useful when you are skilled in the area you are managing. There are several issues with relying on this heavily in the long term:

- You stunt the growth of your people. You will tend to only retain people who are unskilled or lazy, and lose your good people. Hint: this is really bad!
- It is difficult to remain the expert without doing the work regularly. And if you're still doing the work, why do you need your staff at all?
- You are unable to move into other manager positions. As a result, you stunt your own growth as a manager.

3. Pathos is the 'appeal to emotion.' This is your relationship power. It is the most effective mode of persuasion. It is also the hardest to build, and the easiest to lose.

So how do we build good relationships? ITIL 2011 edition describes a lifecycle with several elements of a good service provider-customer relationship. They are also applicable to your relationship with your direct reports. Here are a few notable items.

Strategy: Define outcomes

Your people are just like you. They have a picture of success they wish to realize. Your people are also not like you. Their statements of success will not match yours.

What to do? You could buy more copies of this book and ask them to do the *Chapter 1* action plan. (My publisher would really appreciate it!) A better approach is to build a great relationship. Get to know them. What do they want for their family? Where do they want their career to go? How do they prefer to interact with others? Think about it this way:

- A master carpenter knows her tools and resources well, so she can get the most out of them.
- A manager's primary resources are her people.
- Thus, a great manager must know her resources (aka her people) well.

Every relationship you have depends on two factors. The first is *how often* you communicate with others. The second is *how useful* your communications are to them. Follow these guidelines:

1. Meet with your people regularly. *Manager-Tools.com* recommends a 30 minute weekly meeting. The agenda is ten minutes for them, ten minutes for you, ten minutes for the

future. You can do it at your desk, over the phone, or at a coffee shop. It is simple, and it works.

2. Listen to your people when they talk. Put down your phone. Close your laptop. Smile. Take notes. Ask them to explain when you don't understand. Let them finish talking.

Do these things, and you will know what matters to your people.

Design: Ensure appropriate customer involvement in design activities

Your people want to have a say in their work. In *Drive*, Daniel Pink identified autonomy, mastery, and purpose, as the three factors in motivation. All of these depend on treating your staff as more than a 'pair of hands.' You can involve them in several ways:

- Ask them to meet with customers and internal stakeholders to get their input.
- Have them gather current state information – documentation, reports, observations, etc.
- Based on what you have learned about their interests, give them elements of planning that will use their skills and/or help them grow.
- Get staff to identify risks and the odds they will turn into issues.
- Let them come up with ways to measure value created for stakeholders.

Transition: Awareness of known errors

Your people depend on you for information. We have all wasted time and energy that could have been saved with timely information. Managers tend to fall into two camps:

1. Only pass along information when instructed to do so.
2. Forward everything with 'FYI' stuck to the top of it.

Neither approach works well. Recall the two factors for good relationships – frequency and usefulness. You may only receive information, *but your team needs knowledge*. Good managers provide information when they know it, with the context to help their people understand and use it.

- How does this affect their daily work?

- Are there new opportunities that may be of interest to them?
- What effect does this news have on their future?
- Does this demonstrate cultural norms that the team needs to be aware of?

This is even more valuable when the information is negative. Your staff will find out if you don't share news with them. And they will assume the worst if you don't set the scene.

Operation: Escalate

Your people want to help make things better. Once they know you are listening, they will let you know what is reducing their ability to deliver value. It is your job to mitigate these issues! Your staff deserve the same courtesy you would extend to any customer needing help:

- Empathize with them. Even if you don't think their issue is that important, to them it is. Ask questions, until you can explain their concern as well as they can.
- Ask them for their ideas on how to fix it **after** they describe the issue. Many managers tell their people not to bring them a problem without a solution. Don't do this. The impulse is admirable – you do want your people to find ways to overcome their issues. The downside is that it reduces the chances you will hear about an issue affecting your team.
- Tell them what you plan to do to address their concern. Start with a general description, and provide more detail if asked.
- Do what you say you are going to do. Nothing destroys relationships faster than not keeping your word.
- Update them regularly on progress, and ask them if anything has changed. The issue may have been overcome by events, and is no longer a concern. It may also have increased in importance and require more urgency.
- Be candid about the results. Tell your people the facts and reasons as best you can.

One important note related to this: it is tempting to try to separate yourself from negative decisions. Resist this impulse. **To your people, you are the company.** When you try to separate yourself from company decisions, your direct reports don't feel close to you. They get worried and confused. Don't put them in a position where they have to choose between doing what they think you want, and what they think the company wants.

When you do this well, you will increase the loyalty and commitment of your team members. You are also modeling how to effectively address customer issues.

Improvement: Customer satisfaction surveys

Your people are a reflection of your ability to manage. Ask them regularly how they feel about the work, the team, and the organization. Write this data down, and track it over time.

Do your people feel 'in the dark'? Do they think the organization cares about them? How they feel about the organization is how they feel about you. This is valuable input for your personal improvement plans.

It also helps with succession planning. Your organization expects your team to maintain their services. If a direct report is unhappy, they are at risk of leaving. Knowing this sooner helps you reduce disruptions. You may even avoid them entirely if you can address the issue!

All of these ideas also apply to your peers. Since you don't have role power with them, pathos (relationship power) is crucial. If your team is large, focus on a few key people and build good relationships with them. You can never have too many people on your side!

As mentioned at the start of the chapter, success consists of both relationships AND results. *Chapter 7* dives into how service catalog management thinking can help your team deliver great results.

Action plan
- Set up weekly meetings with your direct reports and peers to get to know them
- Involve them in work that matters to them
- Give them the knowledge they need to be successful
- Understand and work on their concerns
- Ask them how things are going regularly

CHAPTER 7: BUILDING YOUR TEAM'S SERVICE CATALOG

'If a man does not know to what port he is sailing, no wind is favorable.' – Socrates

Most IT staff do not know how they add value. They can tell you what they do. They may even know who they do it for. But their why statements often sound like this:

- 'I just do what they tell me'
- 'Because someone has to do this'
- 'Get the work out the door as fast as possible'

When someone does not see how they add value, they narrow their focus. They try to make their job better, with little regard for how it impacts others. Processes become shortcuts. Quality falls to minimal levels. Customers get more obstacles up-front in the name of efficiency. The result is poor service and a toxic workplace.

How can you provide your direct reports with a holistic picture of the value chain? By showing how their work contributes to the success of the enterprise. ITIL's guidance on service catalog management can help you do this.

The service catalog's primary purpose is to tell customers what services they can use, and how to get them. Yet a service catalog also shows what elements come together to make up a service. This info provides the context your staff needs to understand their value. Here is one way to use service catalog management thinking to meet this need.

Define the services your team provides

The guidance from *Chapter 2* is as valid for your team as it is for yourself. Invest the time and energy to define your team's services. Include your staff in the process.

'But we're all too busy,'! you may say. Yes, this is not easy to do in today's workplace. Everyone has work piled up to their ears. You have imminent deadlines. Yet this is an investment that pays for itself quickly. Consider this:

- Employees that understand why their work matters are more engaged than those who don't.
- Engaged employees are more productive.

Break the work up. Spend one hour a week on it if you must. But don't ignore it.

Identify the activities your team members perform

Everyone is busy. Do not mistake this for value. It is easy to spend your time on tasks that are not valued by customers. While some of these items are necessary, you want your team to focus its energy on what is valued.

Have each of your staff tell you what their primary tasks are. You will be surprised at what you hear! Don't try to correct them on what they should be doing at this point. Just listen and take notes. To keep your poise, ask yourself if your boss would be just as shocked to find out how you spend your time each day.

Determine the links between your team's activities and services

For each of your team's activities, identify the service they help deliver. Your best aid to do this will be the processes in your service designs. You will be able to classify items into two states:

Activities clearly linked to services

These items have value. Make sure each of your direct reports that carry out these tasks understand this relationship. It will not only deliver better results, it will also help them see the purpose in their work.

Activities that do not support a defined service

Examine each activity and ask yourself two questions. Who do we do this for? Why do we do it? There are several possibilities:

- *You missed defining a service that your team delivers.* Perhaps a team member is still doing work from their last job. Maybe one of your staff has a unique skill leveraged by others. Review this item and work with the stakeholders to either formalize it, move it, or retire it.

- *Your team is helping deliver a broader service.* Good news – you've identified another way your team helps others! Work with the service stakeholders to understand its value. Share your findings with your team, so they can see why this work matters.
- *The work is necessary to keep the organization going.* Lean thinking defines certain tasks as necessary non-value adding (NNVA). Larger organizations have more, due to the need for greater coordination. Find ways to minimize time and effort to deliver what is needed. Help your people understand why this work is required. And if you don't understand the value, ask around – perhaps the activity needs to be stopped!
- *The work does not add value.* Ask your team member to stop doing the activity for one month. They will have concerns. Perhaps it used to be required. Maybe they feel others **should** value the work but it only matters to them. Note their concerns and have them stop anyway. You can always have them start again, if needed, after the month is up.

Once you know your team's services, it is important to manage the suppliers of those services – your staff! You can use ITIL's supplier management process to manage the lifecycle of your staff's skills.

Establish your team's skill standards

Be clear on what you want from your people. What skills are needed to provide your team's services? Make sure to include so-called 'soft skills.' Negotiation, public speaking, business writing, and other abilities, are essential for nearly every office job.

Consult your team job descriptions. Do they match the list above? If not, update them. They help you in all phases of the employee lifecycle.

Evaluate and acquire new team members

Hiring is the most important thing you do as a manager. Let me repeat that: *hiring is the most important thing you do as a manager!* When you have great team members, everything else is much easier. Bad hires can derail your services – and your career.

Use these tips to increase your odds of making good hiring choices.

- *Study interviewing* – Most people think they are good interviewers. Nearly all of them are wrong. Take advantage of training offered by your enterprise. Be aware that they tend to focus on avoiding HR issues. You need more than that! Behavioral interviewing is a proven approach to reduce the odds of a bad hire. A great place to start is *Hire With Your Head* by Lou Adler.
- *Practice your skills* – Offer to help interview candidates for other teams. Not only does this earn you favor with your peers; it lets you practice with lower stakes.
- *Keep your standards high* – When you are short staffed, it is tempting to hire quickly. Avoid this impulse. If you have doubts about a candidate, do not hire them. The worst thing you can do is make a bad hire. Do not settle until you find someone that has the skills, team fit, and energy, to be successful.

Manage your team

Managing people is not complex. It is also not easy. You have to do the behind-the-scenes work that sets your people up for success. Make time for these activities:

- Daily
  - o Provide performance feedback (*see Chapter 10* for more specific guidance)
  - o Talk to each of your direct reports, even if only for a minute
- Weekly
  - o Meet with your people one-on-one (*see Chapter 6* for more specific guidance)
  - o Conduct staff meetings
- Bi-weekly
  - o Meet with key peers one-on-one (weekly if possible)
- Monthly
  - o Host staff meetings with the direct reports of your managers (if you are a manager of managers)
- Quarterly
  - o Review each staff member's performance with them
  - o Perform continuity planning for each of your team members
  - o Assess and update team services

You may balk at the above list. You are not just managing; you have to do actual work too! Be assured that every item on this list will save you time, energy, and credibility, in the long run. Schedule recurring time on your calendar to do these items, even if you cannot start until a month from now. That is better than not doing them at all!

Like all other good management practices, make sure you revisit these topics regularly. It is easy to drift into work habits that appear useful – but aren't. Also, you must keep up with changes in your organization. In *Chapter 8* we will examine how change and configuration management practices can help your team mitigate risks.

Action plan

- Define your team's services and assess their activities
- Regularly talk with your team about how their work supports the organization
- Develop your interview skills
- Schedule time to manage your people

CHAPTER 8: MAINTAINING TEAM ASSETS THROUGH EFFECTIVE CONFIGURATION AND CHANGE MANAGEMENT

'If you cry "forward," you must, without fail, make plain in what direction to go.' – Anton Chekhov

Few things are more frustrating than not having the tools needed to do the job well. Over half of all employees who do not feel they have access to the systems needed for their work, report being overstressed. You play a central role in making sure your team has the assets they need to succeed.

ITIL calls any asset used to deliver a service a Configuration Item (CI). Since your staff's tools enable them to be successful, they can be considered CIs for your team's services. That means the processes that focus on CIs can help you address your team's needs. In this chapter we will review how Service Asset and Configuration Management (SACM), Change Management, and Change Evaluation guidance, can help you.

The SACM process, defined by ITIL, focuses on control of CIs. It defines five activities that we will use as our overall process.

Manage and plan CIs

Start by creating your overall plan for managing your team's CIs. Here are some simple rules to get started:

- All CIs must have a home (physical or virtual)
- All CIs must have an owner
- All CIs must be reviewed regularly
- All CIs must have a unique identifier
- All CIs must have documentation that lists each of the above items, along with what team services they enable
- CI documentation must be kept up to date

Your document does not have to be fancy – a spreadsheet is fine for this. You can even list the document IN your document, if you want to be thorough!

Configuration identification

The list of your team's services you created in *Chapter 7* is a huge help here. For each team service, ask your staff what tools they use. Include devices, books, applications, files, and documents, to start. Combine the lists and have your direct reports review it. You will often find immediate value from your team members learning about tools others use to do the same job!

Take time to observe your team's work. You will often see them using documents and tools not listed. It is easy to miss job aids and personal notebooks because they become a habit that does not require thought. Doing this also reduces the odds of missing 'secret' resources that staff may not be sharing with others.

Review your completed list of tools and determine how important they are to your team's services. Are you unable to deliver your services without it? Would a staff member be unable to work? Would you be unable to keep your commitments? Document each item that meets one or more of these criteria in your list of CIs. Other items can be set aside for now and added later if needed.

You will want to track additional information for some of your items. For example, you may want to record the version number and license ID for software CIs. While a few data points are fine, be careful not to try to do too much. Sustaining your tracking is essential.

Control configuration

Like other IT services, the biggest threat to your team's service delivery is poorly handled changes to your CIs. A lost book. A deleted file. A failed software update. They disrupt your team and impact your stakeholders.

Start by deciding what changes are in scope for each CI. *Table 3* outlines some good rules to start:

Table 3: Asset types

Asset Type	In Scope for Control	Out of Scope for Control
Shared Assets	Changing locations (physical/virtual), removing content, modifying structure, changing owners, depleting a supply (e.g. taking the last batch of printer paper)	Using the asset, adding log entries, making copies
Individual Assets	Using an asset assigned to others, changes that make the asset unusable by others (e.g. tearing pages from a book), non-standard personal use	Using the asset, creating derivative works, adding notes

With the scope defined, ITIL's change management process can help manage control. Start by defining standard changes for each CI. Keep it simple. For instance, anyone who borrows a reference book must sign it out. The goal is not to eliminate risk but to balance risk with delivering value. Putting a $10,000 item under lock and key makes sense. Locking up a replaceable $1 book does not.

For in-scope changes, everyone (including you!) should follow a defined process. For instance, let's say someone wants to centralize all your team's reference materials in one place.

- Document the proposed change and assign it a unique ID. What materials are moving? Where will they go? When do we want to make the change? Who will do the work? Why should we do this? What are the risks? An hour of work by a staff member after hours is very different from a week lost while another team packs and moves your items.

- Assess and evaluate the change. Use ITIL's change evaluation process to help you with this for riskier changes. In this example, a simpler approach is fine.
  o Identify which services depend on the items that will be moved.
  o Ask each team member identified with these services about any risks they see.
  o Assess the risk to each service. What is the worst-case scenario? What would you do if that happened? If you can live with that, the risk is manageable.
  o How do the costs and benefits compare? You only need a good enough estimate to make a decision on whether to proceed.

- Build and test the change. Take a couple of books to the new location. Have each person try to get to them. While this may sound silly, don't overlook this! What if a team member does not have permission to access the new location? What if they cannot physically access the space? Does it take too long to get there? What is the backout plan, and does it work? For bigger changes, consult ITIL's service validation and testing process for more ideas.

- Authorize the change. Notify stakeholders, and determine exactly when to do the work. Tell your staff about the change in multiple ways – email, team meetings, one-on-one. Over-communicate. A few wasted seconds is far better than lack of awareness.

- Perform the change. Make sure everyone knows when they should stop and use the backout plan. Ensure the team notifies stakeholders appropriately when the change begins and ends.

- Review the change. Use a Post-Implementation Review (PIR) to ensure work was done as expected. Were all steps completed? Did any surprises occur? Are there any ideas for improvements? Be sure to praise and reward good work as well.

Perform status accounting and reporting

As changes are made to the CIs, ensure that documentation is updated. The simplest way to do this is to record the change ID in your documentation, and update it. If you are using a more complex tool, it may be able to create a relationship between the asset and the change record. Without this work, your documentation will become inaccurate which reduces the value of having it.

Verify and audit

Check your CI entries regularly for any gaps. Many people perform audits every three or six months. You can also include this at the start of every change assessment, and when an incident occurs with a CI. If a difference is found (e.g. a file has been moved), consult change records for any missed updates.

If you can't find documentation for the variation, it is usually best to change the system back to match your records. This reduces the incentive to make unauthorized changes.

By using this approach, you increase your staff's satisfaction and engagement. They can focus on their primary means of adding value – delivering on requests. In *Chapter 9* you will learn how request fulfillment thinking can maximize your team's value and consistency, regardless of their work.

Action plan

- Identify and document the assets that support your team's services
- Manage changes to those assets
- Validate your team's service assets regularly

CHAPTER 9: STREAMLINING TEAM WORKFLOW WITH REQUEST FULFILLMENT

'What is important is seldom urgent and what is urgent is seldom important.' – Dwight D. Eisenhower

Your team is asked to do many things. Attend meetings. Submit time sheets. Produce reports. Perform their jobs! All of these items can be considered requests. The goal is to complete requests on time, on budget, and with high quality.

What happens when you get an urgent request for assistance from your team? Do they push back because they are busy? You don't want to say 'no,' yet you also don't want to overwhelm your team. How can you help your people prioritize their work and ensure important things get done?

ITIL calls this kind of work a service request. It defines a service request as 'a formal request from a user for something to be provided.' ITIL v3 introduced the request fulfillment process to manage service requests. You can use its guidance to improve your team's ability to deliver on its work in four simple steps.

1. Rank your team's services and other assigned work

You defined your team's services in *Chapter 7*. Now you need to order them by their value. Keep it simple.

- High – It directly affects the enterprise's customers and/or other external stakeholders (regulators, etc.)
- Medium – It enables internal staff to do work that directly supports customers and/or other external stakeholders
- Low – Everything else

Put each service in one of these groups. If you're not sure, consider these questions:

- Is it on your performance plan?
- Do you regularly provide status updates on it?
- How often is it used?
- If you stopped doing it, how long would it be before others noticed?

2. Define request models for your team's most important services

A request model is a pre-defined way to handle a type of request. Creating these models provides several benefits:

- More consistent results
- Simpler training
- Useful measurement and reporting
- Easier improvement

For your highest priority service, identify the most common types of requests. Build a model for each request type by defining how to do each step of ITIL's request fulfillment process:

- **Receive request:** Identify the allowed channels. Are requests by phone allowed? By email? Walk-ups?
- **Validate request:** Determine who can make the request. Can only employees make the request? Is it limited to certain job titles?
- **Log and categorize request:** Define recording standards. Should every request be in a spreadsheet? An ITSM tool? What format should be used for data entry? What types of data should be captured?
- **Prioritize the request:** Should the work be done immediately? Should it go on top of the stack of work to be done next? Or does it go to the bottom?
- **Authorize the request:** Specify any approval(s) needed. How can they be given? Are there pre-approved guidelines that can be used, instead of waiting for an approval?
- **Execute the request:** Call out the process flow. What steps must be executed? What roles are involved? Who plays those roles? Is there work required outside your team?
- **Close the request:** How is the requester informed of completion? What other milestones should be communicated? What mediums (phone, email, etc.) are allowed?

Your model should also specify how to log when each step is performed. Check your models by watching someone else do the work. Make updates, and check them with other team members.

3. Set up training and monitoring on your models

Unused models are worthless. Sending your team an email is not training. Neither is posting a document on a website. Adult learners need an overview, an example, and a practice area. Over-invest in this, especially for your first few models.

You must also track usage of the models. Start with reporting on a few measures.

- How many records are created for each model?
- How long do they take to complete?
- Are they recorded correctly?

4. Regularly review, refine, and add to your models

Your initial reports will often show you issues you were not aware of. **Do not** use them as a reason to punish your staff. Execution gaps at the start are expected! When you find problems, go see what is causing them. The root cause is typically one of three things:

1. Inadequate training
2. Vague documentation
3. Unclear expectations and/or understanding

None of these items can be fixed by threats and pressure! Use the 5 Whys to move past blame, and focus on fixing issues.

Take complaints sincerely. Use them to drive improvements. But don't limit yourself. Use other ways to get input on how you are doing. Ask your key stakeholders and requesters for their thoughts. Are they using your services differently? If so, your priorities may need to change.

Create new models when warranted. A good target is to have models in place for all your high value services and your most frequent medium and low value services. This helps you balance the value you get from request models, with the effort required to maintain them.

Great relationships, value-defined services, useful tools, and clear expectations, are crucial to a high performance team. Yet they are not enough to sustain success. The missing ingredient is clear, consistent feedback. In *Chapter 10* we will examine how the CSI model can help keep your team on track.

Action plan

- Rank your services
- Define models
- Train your team

CHAPTER 10: IMPROVING TEAM PERFORMANCE WITH MONITOR CONTROL LOOPS

'Feedback is the breakfast of champions.' – Ken Blanchard

Do you remember trying to learn to ride a bicycle? Perhaps you started out with training wheels. They kept you from falling while you got familiar with pedaling and steering. At some point, someone took them off, so you could learn how to balance. Each time you fell, you learned what not to do – until you were able to stay up!

The same ideas apply to your team. You, as the manager, must let your team members know how they are doing. If you don't, they will develop slowly – if at all. *Feedback is CSI for your team's performance.* It is also an important service you deliver for your organization. But there are many pitfalls – see *table 4*:

Table 4: Feedback pitfalls

Pitfall	Risk
Focusing on judgments instead of behaviors	You can only effectively observe and provide feedback on behaviors
Only telling people when they mess up	Demotivating; drives many workers to not want to do anything at all
Only telling people when they do well	Staff will repeat their mistakes and may become less tolerant of listening to advice on improvement
Vague comments	Team members will misunderstand and make undesired changes
Public feedback	Negative public feedback is demoralizing; positive public feedback is uncomfortable for many people as well

Even avoiding these mistakes is not enough. Most managers do not understand an essential truth: **it is impossible to change the past**. This accounts for the two most common issues with feedback:

1. Giving feedback when it will not be heard.
   When your direct report is upset or embarrassed, they will be defensive. When they are defensive, they are not listening to learn. If they are not listening to learn, feedback is worthless!

2. Focusing on the incident instead of what to learn from it.
   When providing corrective feedback, your staff member is worried. After all, you're the boss! It is logical that they will want to explain what happened. Their focus is to show why what happened was not their fault. It is easy for your feedback to turn into an investigation. Resist this urge! There is no value in assigning fault. There *is* value in helping your team member learn from it for the future.

Fortunately, ITIL provides a very useful structure for feedback. While technically part of the ITIL Service Operation book, the monitor control loop is also referenced in CSI – see *figure 2*.

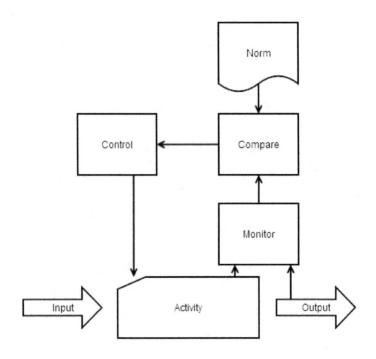

Figure 2: The monitor control loop

Here is how to apply the monitor control loop to deliver effective feedback to your team.

Step 1: Define the desired norm and output

Before you can give helpful feedback, you must define what 'good' looks like. Define the behaviors you want. Manager Tools defines five types of behavior you can observe:

1. Words used
2. How they were communicated (tone, pitch, volume, font, etc.)
3. Facial expressions
4. Body language
5. Work products (outcomes)

We do not often think about behaviors. Your brain judges behaviors so quickly, you often cannot even describe them. For example, 'Dave was rude' does not describe behavior, it describes your feelings. 'Dave did not respond when I asked a question' is a behavior.

Become a student of behaviors. Ask yourself what behaviors you exhibit and observe. Document what behaviors lead to good outcomes. What kinds of body language are well received? What words make others angry (and what behaviors make you think they are angry)?

Don't forget about work products! One of the benefits of defining your services, as covered in *Chapter 7*, is having a clear statement of desired outcomes.

Step 2: Tell your team members what outcomes and norms you want

Do you recall a time you offended someone without realizing it? That is how your staff feel when they get a bad outcome and don't know why. Share your expectations with your team at every opportunity. Here are some ideas to get you started:

- Treat everyone with respect and kindness
- Ask for help when you need it
- Do your best
- Meet your deadlines, or communicate early if you can't
- Follow organization principles, policies, and processes
- Be open to feedback, and look for ways to improve

The most powerful form of sharing is leading by example. If you don't want your direct reports to raise their voice with others, don't do it yourself. 'Do as I say, not as I do,' does not work!

Write down your most important norms. Review them with every one of your staff. Tell stories about yourself (good and bad) that reinforce the message.

Step 3: Observe your team's behaviors (Monitor)

Gemba is an important Lean concept. It is a Japanese word that means 'the real place.' For you, gemba is your team's work activities. That's where the value is! Go to meetings and watch your staff work with others. Read their emails and documents.

Tell them why your are observing their work. It is to help them be successful! Don't hide. Don't try to be sneaky. Your people will worry that you are building a case to fire them. This is why building a relationship with them (*Chapter 6*) is so important. Be open about what you are doing.

Take notes. Write down behaviors, not judgments. What words did they say? Did they smile? Roll their eyes? Keep an even tone of voice? Cross their arms? Be specific, and note the consequences.

Step 4: Prepare for feedback (Compare)

Review the behaviors compared to the desired norms and outcomes. Focus on the positives. Managers are taught to focus on negative exceptions. You will get better results emphasizing good behaviors.

Before you deliver feedback, make sure you are in the right mindset.

- Are you angry, stressed or fearful? If so, delay your feedback until you are in a better mood.
- Can you describe the behavior? If you can only state your judgment, review what happened and identify the behavior that led to your assessment.
- What were the consequences? You need to be able to link the behavior to the result.

- Have you shared your expectations about the behavior? If not, make a note to share this norm with all of your staff, in addition to the feedback.
- Can you deliver it in a non-public environment? Feedback of any kind in front of others is rarely helpful. A side conversation in a meeting is fine. So is delivering it while walking with your direct report to a meeting.

Do not give feedback until you can deliver it calmly, factually, and helpfully.

Step 5: Deliver feedback (Control)

It takes practice to get good at feedback. You want to be brief, be heard, and be focused on the future. The best approach to use is the feedback model recommended by Manager Tools (*www.manager-tools.com*). Their model has been used by thousands of managers to improve their team's performance. It consists of four steps:

1. *Ask if the person is ready for feedback.* Use a phrase, such as 'May I give you some feedback'? or 'Can I share something with you'? This may seem odd, yet it is critical. Remember that the purpose of feedback is to affect the future. If your team member is thinking about other things and does not hear you, your feedback is useless! Even if the feedback is affirming, if they are not ready, wait until another time.
   If you're worried about doing this, keep the following points in mind:
   - Behaviors happen all the time. If you miss an opportunity to deliver feedback, another chance will happen soon.
   - If the behavior needs correction, one of two things will happen:
     1. The behavior will happen again, and you will have another chance to give feedback
     2. The behavior won't happen again, which is what you wanted!
   - If a direct report always declines feedback, remind them of your expectations about being open to feedback, and work on your relationship.
2. *Describe the behavior.* Frame your sentence as 'When you,' followed by what you observed. Here are some examples:

- Good descriptions: 'when you publish an agenda for your meeting,' 'when you start talking while I am talking,' 'when you don't make eye contact with your audience,' 'when you contribute ideas about project risks'.
- Not good descriptions: 'when you are rude to people,' 'when you are energetic,' 'when you put others at ease' – these are judgments, not behaviors.

Judgments are often misunderstood and can put people on the defensive. Consider this. If someone told you that you had a bad attitude, what response would you get? 'No, I don't'! Describing behaviors reduces defensiveness. The focus on facts gives your direct report useful, specific areas to improve.

3. *Describe the impact.* Tell your team member the effects of their behavior. For instance, here is how the good example in step 2 could continue:
   - 'When you publish an agenda for your meeting, it helps us prepare, so we don't waste time'.
   - 'When you start talking while I am talking, I feel it is rude and that you are not listening'.
   - 'When you make eye contact with your audience, they are more likely to be persuaded by your ideas'.
   - 'When you contribute ideas about project risks, we are more likely to meet our project goals'.

   The outcomes can be about both results (meeting deadlines, increased revenue, and reduced costs) and relationships. Your staff need feedback in both areas. Note that sharing *your* judgments in this step is fine. After all, you are an authority on how you feel!

4. *Influence future behavior.* Wrap up the feedback in one of two ways:
   1. If the feedback was encouraging, tell them 'Thanks.'
   2. If it was corrective, ask them 'Can you change that'?

   Feedback is uncomfortable for you and your direct report. Keep it short. That makes it easier to do. Making it easier helps you do it more often. And the more you do it, the better you will get!

Step 6: Review your performance in giving feedback (monitor control loop)

Take stock of how often you are delivering feedback. Set up a monitor control loop for yourself! Compare it to the following norms:

- Are you providing feedback every day? Target giving one piece of feedback daily. Once you achieve this level for several weeks, increase this by one per day.
- Are you focused on affirming desired behaviors? Target a 5:1 ratio of affirming to adjusting (corrective) feedback.
- How long does it take to deliver feedback? Target an average of 30 seconds. If it is taking longer, you are probably not being specific enough about behaviors in your feedback, or you are taking too long to wrap up.

When you give your direct reports good feedback, they do more of what you want, and less of what you don't want. What could be better than that as a manager?

Managing a team well is hard. We focused on five areas essential for high performance:

1. Build strong relationships with every team member
2. Help direct reports understand why what they do is valuable
3. Ensure your staff have the tools they need to deliver their services
4. Provide clear guidance on how to perform work
5. Give frequent feedback on performance

In Part III we will focus on our boss and other stewards of the enterprise. How can we effectively influence them and help them be successful? Once again, service management thinking gives us several tools we can use.

Action plan

- Define what behaviors you want to see from your team
- Communicate norms and expectations
- Give useful feedback every day

PART III – EFFECTIVENESS WITH LEADERS

'The greatest ability in business is to get along with others and to influence their actions.' – John Hancock

Influence matters. Conflict is inevitable. Compliance is not enough. The 'yes man' has no future. Power flows through networks. Today's leader builds coalitions, not walls.

CHAPTER 11: APPLYING SERVICE PORTFOLIO THINKING TO INFLUENCE LEADERS

'You've got to think about big things while you're doing small things, so that all the small things go in the right direction.'
– Alvin Toffler

Have you ever worked for a boss that would not listen to your ideas? Perhaps you were new to the workforce and they had been around forever. Maybe they didn't listen to anyone else, either. Regardless, there are few things more frustrating than having a great idea that goes nowhere.

Your ability to influence enterprise decisions starts by building relationships with your leaders. The principles in *Chapter 6* can help you do this. You must also deliver results. But this is not enough! You must also be able to speak their language. This is foreign to most technology people, but ITSM principles can help.

ITIL defines a process for making decisions regarding IT services as service portfolio management (SPM). The service portfolio is the approved set of IT services that the enterprise is willing to invest in. The SPM process consists of four steps. How can this process help you get support for your initiatives? By helping you tweak your ideas and business case to make its value easier for others to see.

Step 1: Define

A tenet of ITSM thinking is that you begin with the end in mind. Influencing decisions is no different. People have reasons for their choices. They may seem crazy, dumb, or short-sighted, to you. Put that aside. After all, have you ever stopped caring about something just because someone else told you not to?

What do your leaders care about? Most people never consider this question. Yet it is powerful. ITSM is all about outcomes, so this is a perfect fit! Learning what matters to your leaders is simple, yet it is not easy. Here are some ways to get insight into their 'hot buttons':

- Ask them! The simplest method, and the hardest for many people, because of their fear. This is another area where a good relationship helps.

- Review recently approved projects. Look for common factors that led to their approval. If you can find documents that describe what criteria are used for project approvals, so much the better.
- Survey key reports used by leaders. 'Used by,' not 'sent to.' Many reports are never looked at, so they will not help you. What kinds of data do the reports show? What questions get asked about reports?
- Look at their presentations. How do they justify decisions? What do they focus on?
- Note questions they ask during meetings, or in messages. Do they always ask about costs? Do certain products, or systems, come up again and again?
- Consult vision, mission, and goal documents. Focus on items that are referenced by leaders. (If your organization has a strategy like the one you created for yourself in *Chapter 1*, use it!)
- Pay attention to announcements. Is there a spending freeze? What big initiative is everyone talking about? Has your enterprise been in the news?

Certain criteria will always come up. Costs, risks, and quality, matter to nearly everyone. Create a list of five to ten items that seem most important. Try to define them. What risks matter? How do you judge quality?

For extra credit, try to rank them in importance to your leaders. This 'lens' will help you think more like an executive when looking at your ideas.

Step 2: Analyze

Evaluate your ideas against each of the criteria specified in step 1. Keep it simple for now. One way is to use a five tier scale, such as in the following example in *table 5*:

Table 5: Sample idea comparison

	Costs	Revenue	Compliance	Risk	Quality	Employee impact
Idea 1	–	0	+	–	++	++
Idea 2	–	+	0	–	+	0

Which idea is better? Often, it will be apparent just from this basic analysis. Sometimes, it is not. Here are some techniques that may help:

- Set it aside and come back to it later
- Describe the ideas to anyone who will listen, even a pet (you may be surprised how often this works!)
- Ask for a second opinion
- Try to combine your ideas into a better idea
- If you're still undecided, flip a coin and move on

Once you have selected an idea, do a more detailed analysis of each factor. Here are some guidelines:

- Check with your finance department for guidelines on how to justify investments. Make a friend in finance, and ask for help if needed.
- For numbers, such as costs, an order of magnitude estimate ($1,000/$10,000/$100,000) is adequate for now.
- For all items, state the benefits and drawbacks as clearly as possible:
  o 'Employees will have clear expectations on what they should do'
  o 'This will address three concerns mentioned in our last audit'
  o 'The change will correct an error that caused over 300 calls to our service desk last week'

It is easy to fall into the trap of only looking at supporting evidence. Before moving on, take ten minutes and identify the biggest drawbacks to your proposal. If you don't, someone else will. Is it still a good idea?

Step 3: Approve

Once you have vetted your idea, you need to create your business case. ITIL describes a business case as 'justification for a significant item of expenditure.' Its purpose is to help decision makers have the facts they need to make the best choice. If your organization has a business case format, start there. If not, make sure you include these items:

- **A clear problem statement.** What is the situation? What are you trying to fix? Hint: if it doesn't relate to one of the criteria in step 1, stop now!

- **Options considered.** There are always alternatives. Otherwise, why would you need a decision? List at least two other options and briefly describe them. Don't forget that not making a change is an option. Include it. This helps reduce the odds that no decision will be made.

- **Criteria used.** The audience needs to know what factors you considered. If they are only focused on one or two items, this helps them see the bigger picture.

- **Comparison of options.** Summarize each option's impact on the criteria. Be candid about each option. Any gain in persuasion from shading the truth will be lost if your credibility is questioned.

- **Your recommendation.** This is scary for many people. Be confident in your analysis! You did your homework. You have focused on what matters. You evaluated each option impartially. You've earned the right to make your recommendation.

- **Expected benefits.** What value will the enterprise get from this effort? Focus on the criteria most important to your leaders. Remember to focus on what's in it for them. Check each item with the 'so what'? test. Read each item and ask yourself 'so what'? Answer the question and repeat until you have an answer that will connect with your audience.

- **Costs.** Nothing is free. Even 'free' projects have costs in time, attention, and resources. Provide order of magnitude estimates on what is needed to be successful. It is hard to get resources at this stage. But it is harder to get them once you've already started!

- **Risks.** All choices have risks, including the status quo. List the most important ones you can think of, and the consequences if they occur. Include ways to minimize, or avoid, the worst risks. Do not leave them out – your audience will assume you have blinders on. They will be less likely to agree to your proposal.

- **High-level time line.** You won't have all the answers at this point. You still need to provide some idea of when key (three to seven) milestones will be reached.

Meet with the decision maker(s) and key stakeholders, one-on-one, to review your case. Get their feedback. Make changes to address their concerns. Be flexible on how you do the work. *Your goal is to achieve the desired outcome, not to do it 100% your way.* This is organizational change management at its core. It is better to get commitment to 70% of your intent than to get tolerance of 100%!

Submit your proposal for formal approval once you have informal agreement. Congratulations, your odds of success are strong, due to your preparation!

Step 4: Charter

Once you have an approved proposal, the real work can begin. Make your stakeholders aware of the decision. Use every channel you can – meetings, email, online systems, etc. Tailor your message to the audience. Do they just need to be aware? Who needs in-depth understanding?

If you now have an approved project, you will be happy for about ten seconds before worry sets in! Even with your preparation, there are many possible pitfalls. Project management is a critical skill for all managers (as discussed in *Chapter 18*). It is straightforward, yet requires influencing skills and attention to detail.

Regardless of whether your proposal was approved, the last step is to review what you learned during this process. Here are some questions to consider:

- Which elements worked well?
- How strong are your relationships with the people involved?
- Did criteria come up that were not on your list?
- Have stakeholder priorities changed?
- What questions were asked about your analysis?
- Were parts of your business case missing or unclear?

Make changes based on what you learn. Don't be discouraged if your idea was not approved. The only truly bad outcome is not learning how to improve!

What comes to mind when you see the word 'politics'? Nothing good, if you are like most people. Yet politics is inevitable in organizations. People have different desires. Politics is how we work through differences to make decisions.

You can be effective at politics and still sleep at night. Focus on your goals. Consider the needs of others. Adjust your course as you learn more. You will have more influence and help your enterprise make better decisions!

Influence is also important in our day-to-day activities. In *Chapter 12* we will look at how service level management ideas can help us set leader expectations – and meet them.

Action plan

- Build relationships with leaders and deliver results
- Identify your organization's decision criteria
- Learn how to analyze ideas based on those criteria

CHAPTER 12: NEGOTIATING WHAT IS EXPECTED OF YOU LEVERAGING SERVICE LEVEL MANAGEMENT PRINCIPLES

'You do not get what you want. You get what you negotiate.'
– Harvey Mackay

Have you ever agreed to something that you later found you could not achieve? Not meeting commitments destroys your reputation. It ruins relationships. Many people try to avoid commitments because of these risks.

Unfortunately, this creates different issues. Would you trust a babysitter unwilling to commit to keeping your children safe while you were away? We want assurance from our service providers. 'Satisfaction guaranteed' is a powerful phrase for a reason.

Another challenge is that there are **always** expectations. Consider walking into a diner. What do you expect, even if you've never eaten there before? Clearly marked prices. Clean dishes. Furniture!

How do we deal with this dilemma? ITIL recommends negotiating agreements through a process called Service Level Management (SLM). Its aim is to help IT work more effectively with business partners. These same tools and techniques can help us manage the expectations of our leaders. In this chapter we will use a four step approach to apply SLM thinking in this area.

Step 1: Determine what your boss and other leaders want from you

Good negotiation starts by understanding what others desire. As discussed in *Chapter 11*, learning what your leaders care about is essential. Start by figuring out what you and your team do that is valuable to your boss. How much? How fast? How good?

The following methods can help you learn more:

- Ask! Again, this (*and everything else with negotiation*) is much easier if you have built a good relationship with your boss (consult *Chapter 6* for ways to do this).
- Review your job description. It is likely to be poorly written and obsolete. Regardless, it was what was expected from your role

at one time. Use it as a check to ensure you don't miss anything that may haunt you later.

- Look at the reports and information requested by your boss. Bosses do not tend to ask for things they don't care about.
- Figure out your boss' goals and what she is being measured on.

Apply these same ideas to any other leaders as appropriate. Don't forget your boss' peers and your boss' boss. They are not only stakeholders, they can also provide growth opportunities for you and your team.

Step 2: Understand what you, and your team, can deliver

Identify the primary constraint for each of your services (consult *Chapter 7* and *8* for more information). This is based on the Theory of Constraints (ToC) by Eli Goldratt. Goldratt showed in his book, *The Goal*, that our output is limited by our bottlenecks and limits. For instance, your primary constraint for providing phone support could be the number of analysts on your team. It could also be the number of phone lines in the phone system. There may even be a limit on the number of licenses you have for troubleshooting software.

Two kinds of CIs warrant close attention:

1. *CIs supplied by third parties outside your enterprise.* ITIL's SLM process refers to agreements with third parties related to IT services as Underpinning Contracts (UCs). The classic example of a UC is a company that provides on-site support. Don't commit to restoring an IT service in four hours if your supplier has six hours just to show up!

2. *CIs that require help from other areas of your enterprise.* ITIL's SLM process recommends having Operating Level Agreements (OLAs) between areas that work together to deliver an IT service. OLA examples include response time for requests, when updates will be provided, and what information and training will be provided during deployments. Again, base your commitments on what your partners can deliver, not wishful thinking.

Once identified, you can then identify ways to address the constraint, if needed. Could you redeploy people or tools from another area that is not constrained, if needed? What about training if you are limited by expertise? Try to identify at least one option that doesn't involve spending more money.

If you are worried that your services will not meet your leader's needs, find other options. What would it cost to get the service from another part of the organization? What third party options exist? Gather information on these services, and their costs and risks.

Why is this important? It gives you more options for meeting the needs you discovered in step 1. You will also be able to explain why you are unable to meet some needs without drastic changes.

Armed with this information, you can then determine the amount of each service your team can reasonably deliver. Your standard offering would be what you can deliver today with no changes.

Step 3: Come to an agreement on expectations

You are ready to negotiate. But first, you may be wondering how you can negotiate at all. Can't your boss just make you do whatever they want anyway? After all, you're not in charge, they are!

You **always** have the option to negotiate. No one else can make you do anything. You may not like the consequences of a choice, yet you always have one! This does not mean you should yell, pound the table, or 'act tough.' You should be polite and friendly. You should also be assertive and advocate for what you need.

Start by validating that you understand your leader's needs. Ask them to confirm your description of the situation. Work to clarify any areas where you differ.

Once you have a common understanding, review your service offerings with them. Focus on the capabilities you provide and how they will help the leader and enterprise succeed. Let them know the costs and risks of each option, in a way that makes sense to them.

Most of the time this approach will yield a solution that meets their needs, that you can deliver. But what if you get stuck? Try this approach:

- Take a deep breath. Assume that your leader's view is legitimate. Your goal is not to change their mind, it is to find a way to meet their needs.

- Walk through your findings and your assumptions with your leader. Ask them to point out anything that is unclear, or doesn't make sense to them. Often, you will discover that an assumption is no longer true. This is the catalyst for breakthrough solutions!

- Review the options outside your area. Be candid about their benefits and risks. Sometimes just showing these other options will reset expectations to a level you can achieve. If other options can meet their needs, use them! Then, work to incorporate those other options into your services.

- If you determine that additional resources are required to meet their needs, work with your leader to obtain those resources. You will likely need to build a business case for a project or a purchase. Follow your organization's process, or use project management guidance from PMBOK® or PRINCE2®.

- If all else fails, be candid that you cannot deliver to the expectations expressed, and ask for guidance on how to proceed. Work with your boss to address any negative consequences.

Frankly, most people who feel they have been asked to do the 'impossible,' do not understand their leader's real needs. If you have truly done all you can to understand the need and try to meet it, you can sleep with a clear conscious.

While it is rare, if you absolutely cannot reach an agreement, be willing to accept the consequences of not meeting what is being asked of you. While unpleasant, making an agreement you cannot live up to is worse.

Step 4: Report on performance

Do you tend to let your work speak for itself? That is a bad idea for a service provider. Most leaders manage by exception. Therefore, there are only two default modes of thinking:

1. You are being thought of poorly
2. You are not being thought of at all!

Provide regular updates to your leaders on how you are doing. Be transparent – good and bad. Resist the urge to make excuses for your failures. Instead, share what you learned and what will change, to reduce the odds of future issues.

Strive to meet with your key stakeholders monthly, or at worst, once a quarter. This allows you to go beyond your report to understand your leader's mindset. What are they focused on? What keeps them up at night? Use this information to adjust your services, agreements, and reporting.

It is easy to fall into the trap of only doing the minimum expected by your boss. Yet it is a losing strategy. Your work to understand and meet the needs of your leaders will be noticed.

As you practice, you will become a trusted partner. You, and your team, will be known as people who can help leaders create the future. The rewards and opportunities are vast. The way forward is simple, yet not easy. But it is worth it!

Your leader also needs information as things change. In *Chapter 13* we will examine how ITIL's transition planning and support process can help you be an effective communicator and sponsor.

Action plan

- Identify how your team's services are useful to your leaders
- Define levels of service that are valuable and achievable
- Review your performance regularly with your boss and key stakeholders

CHAPTER 13: KEEPING YOUR LEADERS WELL INFORMED USING TRANSITION PLANNING AND SUPPORT THINKING

'Don't tell me about your effort. Show me your results.'
– Tim Fargo

Your leaders hate surprises. Their job is to translate the uncertainty of the world into a clear vision for your enterprise. Information gaps lead to poor decisions and outcomes. That is why sharing your results (as discussed in *Chapter 12*) is essential.

That is only part of the picture. Your enterprise uses projects to reduce waste and improve value. Even if you are an operational manager, you will run projects. For instance, a service desk manager wants to reduce call times and provide better support. This is a deep field, worthy of your attention. *Chapter 18* provides an overview of key elements that can help.

One challenge with projects is that they increase uncertainty. Is the project on schedule? Will we get the value we expected? When leaders don't know how your project is doing, bad things happen. Funding cuts. Last-minute vetoes. Redundant work.

The ITIL Service Transition book[1] emphasizes the value of managing stakeholders and communications. The transition planning and support process can help you avoid communication failures. In this chapter we will use a four-step approach to manage communications with your leaders and other key stakeholders.

Identify the stakeholders for your services and projects

Pull together a list of your team's services (*see Chapter 7* for help on this) and any projects you are working on. Identify the stakeholders for each item. Here are some broad categories to help you get started:

---

[1] Available at *www.itgovernance.co.uk/shop/p-831-itil-2011-service-transition.aspx*.

- Direct reports and other involved staff
- Your chain of command
- Peers, and their teams, that support your work
- Internal and external regulators
- Customers of your services
- Suppliers

For each stakeholder, identify their information needs. What do they need to know? When do they prefer to be updated? What communication channels do they use? As always, the better your relationship with that stakeholder (*Chapter 6*), the more effectively you can meet their needs.

Develop a communication plan that meets your stakeholders' needs. For each message type, decide who will send it, what channel to use, and how often to provide updates. Be cautious about using the exact same message to multiple audiences. After all, if they don't understand you, you've wasted their time – and yours!

Share your communication plan for each stakeholder with them

Remember the first sentence of this chapter? An unexpected status update is a surprise. Don't do it! Let each stakeholder know your communication schedule. Tell them when they will receive updates, and how they will get them.

Ask for feedback from your stakeholders. Are the updates too frequent? Would they prefer them in a different medium? Adjust your plans based on the feedback you receive. You will also get a feel for the level of interest in what you are doing.

- Are unexpected people asking for more frequent updates?
- No response from those you identified as highly impacted?
- Are you getting the same questions from multiple recipients?

Those gaps mean your work's impact is different from what you expected. Resolve them now, or pay for them later!

Communicate per your schedule

As mentioned in *Chapter 12*, not keeping your commitments destroys trust. Block off time to create, and provide, your updates. Otherwise, it may slip your mind, as urgent items come up.

Keep your communications focused, brief, and fact-based. Your leaders are busy. Don't waste their attention on items that don't matter. Follow these guidelines:

- Use an organization-approved format, if there is one, and it is familiar to your audience. If not, create a simple format and use it consistently.

- Make the first thing people see in your update the key takeaway. Don't make your audience search for the message. Otherwise, they will come up with something else. You probably won't like it!

- Be brief. Long updates are as painful to read as they are to write. You can always give more detail when asked.

- 'Fine' is not a status. 'All deliverables on schedule' is a status. 'Quality checks all passed' is a status. 'Fine' is interpreted as 'I have no idea what is going on.'

- If you missed a deadline, or have other bad news, state the news, any impact, and what **you** are doing to minimize the fallout. Don't hide problems. Don't point fingers. When in doubt, take accountability and try to do better next time.

- Call out the good things, too, and the people that helped make them happen. As Hank Marquis says, 'Always share the glory, and always be seen sharing the glory.'

- Don't make stuff up. If you don't know, say so. Commit to follow up once you do know, and ask for help.

Refine and update your communication plan

Keep your plan fresh. Pay attention to comments and concerns. Adjust your timing, content, and medium, as you learn more. Your stakeholders' interests will change. Tailor your updates so they remain relevant and useful.

Take action when there is turnover in your stakeholders. Meet the new person and brief them on what you are doing – and why. Find out how they prefer to get updates. This builds relationships, gets them up to speed faster, and bolsters your reputation to boot.

Finally, update everyone when your projects achieve major milestones and when they finish. Bring your stakeholders together. Call out the benefits gained. Ask for, and share, lessons learned. Celebrate successes! Your project is not done until everyone knows how they can use what was delivered.

Being a good communicator is simple, yet not easy. It requires diligence and preparation. It is often ignored. Doing it well sets you apart from others. It builds relationships and opens doors to opportunity.

Those opportunities are often disguised, though, as problems. In *Chapter 14* we will examine how problem management thinking can help you solve the challenges your leaders face.

Action plan

- Identify the stakeholders of your services and projects
- Develop a communication plan to meet stakeholder needs
- Schedule time to plan, deliver, and improve your communications

CHAPTER 14: MAKE YOUR LEADERS' LIVES EASIER THROUGH STRONG PROBLEM MANAGEMENT

'There is always a well-known solution to every human problem – neat, plausible, and wrong.' – H.L. Mencken

Have you ever played the carnival game Whac-a-mole™? You have a big foam mallet and you use it to hit 'moles' as they pop up from the game board. It starts off easy, but as it gets faster, it is hard to keep up. It is fun, and you can win a stuffed plush bear or some other animal.

Like this game, your leaders expect you to help solve issues the enterprise faces. Eroding margins. Tough competitors. Rising customer expectations. Yet you also need to deal with all sorts of other issues. Under-performing employees. Off-track projects. Vendor delays. Staff conflict. There are a lot of 'moles' – and they often seem to pop up all at once!

Most managers approach these issues like that carnival game. They don't see an issue until it 'pops up' as an outage or complaint. Then they stop what they are doing to 'whack' the 'mole' until the outage or complaint stops. Yet this is only a stopgap. Meanwhile, important work is set aside.

The result? They spend long hours at the office. Their families and friends suffer. Their employees leave. Opportunities (both enterprise and personal) vanish.

The solution is effective problem solving. ITIL's problem management process is an ideal tool to help you do this. It is not just for technical issues! In this chapter, we will apply problem management thinking to show you how to solve and/or prevent the everyday issues you face as a manager.

Problem detection

You can't fix problems until you are aware of them. While obvious, the implications are often missed. *You must find ways to detect potential issues early.* Adopt the motto 'a stitch in time saves nine.' Here are some ideas that can help:

- **Build good relationships with your staff and peers.** Your best early warning system is the people around you. Again, *Chapter 6* provides a good approach to connecting with others. When people feel comfortable sharing their concerns with you, you will be able to see potential issues much sooner.

- **Schedule time to see what is going on.** As mentioned in *Chapter 10*, *gemba* is 'the real place' where work happens. Block off time to observe what is going on around you. Are processes being followed? Does a team member appear stressed or distracted? What are people talking about at lunch, or in the break room? Each workplace has its own rhythm. Learn it, and it will be easier to see when things start to go wrong.

- **Review reports regularly.** While reports can have many issues of their own (as will be discussed in *Chapter 15*), a good report can provide early indicators of issues. Become familiar with your reports. You will begin to see patterns that can alert you to concerns.

- **Keep up with industry news.** You are special, but your problems are probably not. Blogs, articles, and conferences, are just a few resources to consult. They can provide insight into how other people identify and solve problems you may face.

This does take time. Many managers say they do not have time for this. Frankly, they are almost always wrong. Investing in problem detection pays great dividends – *if* you truly fix them.

Problem logging, categorization, and prioritization

This is the most critical step of problem solving. Most people are poor problem solvers. They fix symptoms instead of causes. They introduce worse problems elsewhere. Their solutions cost more than just living with the problem! At the heart of all of these follies is not determining the right problem to solve before trying to fix it.

ITIL suggests an excellent approach, called Kepner-Tregoe, to aid problem analysis. Its first two steps are useful in identifying a problem.

- **Defining the problem.** Lazy problem definition leads to bad outcomes. Start by using the '5 Whys' technique (described in *Chapter 1*) to identify underlying causes. For each potential cause, specify the conditions that lead to the problem. The GQM

(Goal-Question-Metric) approach suggests five parameters that are useful for defining a problem:

1. Object: Pinpoint the person, process, product, tool, or other resource affected by the problem.
2. Purpose/intent: Identify what the problem is preventing. Increased revenue? Reduced cost? Higher retention of customers and/or staff?
3. Focus: List the aspect affected. Is it unreliable? Does it cause delays? Is it unusable?
4. Viewpoint: Specify who is seeing the problem. Is it you? Your staff? A customer? Your boss?
5. Environment: Establish the system and/or service where the problem is observed. Your payroll system? Staff meetings? A specific project?

'Our customer satisfaction scores have dropped,' is a poor problem definition. 'Vending machine purchasers are reporting lower satisfaction with post-sales service on our 90 days after purchase survey,' is much better.

- **Describing the problem.** ITIL's description of Kepner-Tregoe calls out four aspects to describe a problem.

  1. Identity: The problem definition from the prior step.
  2. Location: Where exactly does the problem occur?
  3. Time: What time does the problem occur? How frequently does it occur? Is there a pattern of recurrence?
  4. Size: How much of the system and/or service is affected?

You can then start to determine what differences separate problem areas from non-problem areas. Kepner-Tregoe recommends separating what 'is' from what 'could be but is not.' You can then identify relevant differences and possible changes that created the gap. Use a table to capture information. The following example, in *table 6* below, builds on the prior defined problem.

Table 6: Kepner-Tregoe example

	Identity	Location	Time	Size
Is	Vending machine purchasers are reporting lower satisfaction with post-sales service on our 90 days after purchase survey	Southeast US region	Past two months	All third party sales
Could be but is not	Purchasers of bill changing and ticket redemption machines	Other regions of the US, other countries	Prior two years	Direct to business sales
Relevant differences	Unique mechanism for dispensing product	Some competitors only in this region	None	Third party sales have different service model
Possible changes	Firmware change in control systems last month	Competitor began offering same-day service a year ago	None	Change in third party service provider three months ago

Problem investigation and diagnosis

Good problem descriptions provide a strong foundation for root cause analysis. Often (like in the example above) a good candidate will present itself. If not, this is a good time to use another tool suggested by ITIL known as the Ishikawa diagram (*figure 3* below). It is a structured way to brainstorm possible causes of the problem.

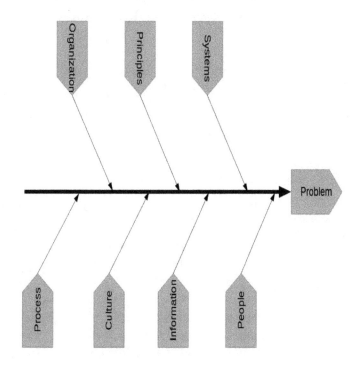

Figure 3: Ishikawa diagram

The COBIT® 5 framework describes seven enablers for IT success (consult *Chapter 20* for more specifics). Using them as your categories helps you to view the problem holistically:

- **Processes** – procedures, work instructions, and other methods
- **Organizational structures** – how decisions are made and by whom
- **Culture, ethics, and behavior** – rewards, punishments, and incentives
- **Principles, policies, and frameworks** – rules and guidelines provided by leadership
- **Information**
- **Services, infrastructure, and applications**
- **People, skills, and competencies**

Focus on each category in turn and identify possible contributors to
the problem. This ensures that you consider the problem from all
aspects. Do not focus on one or two items and begin designing
solutions!

Once you have reviewed each category in turn, analyze each
option with a simple test. Does the option fit the problem definition
and description you created earlier? If not, set it aside and
consider other possible causes. Continue until you have identified
two or three likely candidates.

Problem workaround and resolution

You are finally ready to begin developing solutions to the problem.
Congratulations for resisting the urge to start with this step!
Though tempting, trying to solve a problem you don't understand
is foolish. Starting with this step often makes things worse
because the 'solution' introduces more total pain than it removes!

Most problems have a natural tension. They often require solutions
that take time to implement. Yet they cause pain that needs quick
attention. Poor managers will often put in a 'temporary' fix, yet
never do the hard work to truly solve the problem.

This does not mean you should avoid workarounds. After all,
bandages and duct tape are great tools in the right context! The
key is to use a workaround to buy time to correct the underlying
issue(s). This minimizes the impact of the problem, while reducing
the risk of future recurrence.

Keep these guidelines in mind when attempting to fix a problem:

- Make sure the cost of fixing a problem is not more than the cost
  of the actual problem. Some problems are like wild animals –
  document, study, and explain them, yet don't disturb them or
  you'll be sorry!

- All problem solutions introduce their own potential problems.
  For instance, you buy an alarm clock so you don't oversleep.
  Now you have to make sure the alarm continues to work!
  Understand your solutions and make sure you know their risks.

- Solving a problem is just like any other business decision. You
  must present your case in a way that makes sense to your
  leaders. Use the ideas in *Chapter 11* to evaluate and then sell
  your recommendation.

- All technical and process problems have underlying behavioral and cultural issues. Ignore them at your peril. This is another reason why good managers focus on behaviors (as discussed in *Chapter 10*).
- Problem analysis is useless without good solution execution. Follow through on your plans.

Problem closure

Once you have implemented a solution, verify that the problem has been fixed. Go back to your problem description. Make sure you actually solved the problem you intended to solve. Just because you implemented an action, that does not mean you fixed the problem! In our example above, the problem is only solved when we verify that customer satisfaction scores have gone back up. It is NOT solved just because we met with the service provider and told them about the problem.

It may take you weeks (or even months) to validate that the problem has been solved. If so, schedule time each week to check on the problem status. Update the problem's stakeholders on progress. Set a deadline for when the problem should be reopened.

Do not despair if the problem is still occurring. Often a problem will mask other underlying problems. Resist the urge to go directly to your next candidate. Don't waste what you learned! Use the Kepner-Tregoe and Ishikawa techniques to update your problem analysis. Can you improve your problem description? What additional differences, and possible changes, have you found? Were there issues in executing the solution? Continue until you solve the problem, or find that there is no longer enough value to continue.

Once you confirm the problem is no longer occurring, share the good news! Identify everyone that helped solve the problem. Estimate the value gained from the solution. Get feedback from customers, and others that benefited from the solution. Provide a summary to your boss, and other leaders, of this information.

For big problems, schedule 30 minutes to bring stakeholders together and celebrate (preferably with food and/or beverages!). Give the highest level leader attending an overview of what was accomplished before the meeting. That will enable them to provide meaningful thanks to everyone involved. It improves your team's motivation, your leader's status, and your reputation with everyone involved.

Your ability to solve problems is an essential career skill. The best way to improve is to practice. Use this approach at every opportunity – at work and at home. It will be time consuming at first. With practice, you will be able to take action quickly and confidently.

Problem detection is greatly aided by good reporting systems. In *Chapter 15* we will discuss how to determine what to measure, and how to do so effectively.

Action plan

- Define the top five problems you face in your current role
- Analyze those problems to determine the causes to address
- Identify solutions and implement them

CHAPTER 15: MEASURING YOUR WAY TO CONTINUAL SUCCESS

'When performance is measured, performance improves. When performance is measured and reported back, the rate of improvement accelerates.' – Thomas S. Monson

Reporting is the most misunderstood concept in management today. Pick up the report closest to you right now. What does the report tell you? Why does it exist? For most reports, the answers are 'nothing useful' and 'I don't know'!

Measurement and reporting is powerful when done well. The trick is to understand their purpose and then how to use them effectively. First, you need to understand a few key rules about measures:

- Rule 1: The purpose of measurement is to reduce uncertainty. This concept is the core of the wonderful book *How to Measure Anything* by Douglas Hubbard, which underpins many of the ideas in this chapter. For instance, say you do not know whether the water in a bathtub is at a comfortable temperature for your bath. When you stick your finger in the water, you now know that it is too hot. You decide to add more cold water. Your measurement reduced the risk of burning yourself in the tub!

- Rule 2: The value of measurement comes from improved decision making. Reports can be misused (for distorting the truth, hiding bad news, or the dreaded 'CYA'). Good reports help us make better choices and carry them out more effectively.

- Rule 3: All measures are proxies. They stand in for something else that is more difficult to measure. A sports team's win/loss record is a proxy for how good the team is compared to other teams. IQ is a proxy for intelligence. Profit is a proxy for business health. The quality of the proxy is based on how credible it is and how well it correlates to what it represents.

- Rule 4: All measures can be 'gamed'. They can be manipulated without actually changing what they are supposed to measure. A sports team can cheat. People can study for an intelligence test. Businesses can cut expenses now that will reduce profit later.

- Rule 5: All measures have a life span due to change. The number of telegraphs in a country was once a good measure of its technological progress. That is no longer the case!

When you combine these ideas, one key point emerges. **The Law of Metrics: there is no such thing as the right measure!** Even the best measure can be distorted, and will be useless some day. Once you understand this, you can then start to use metrics well.

ITIL's Continual Service Improvement volume[2] provides a valuable approach for thinking about measures. In this chapter we will look at the four reasons for measurement. Each of them can be aligned to the four stages of Deming's PDCA cycle. Once you identify a measure, you can use the practices in *Chapter 3* to turn them into knowledge that aids your decision making.

Measuring to justify (Plan)

'Just because' is a poor reason to do anything. You must build a case for action. In *Chapter 11* we reviewed the importance of choosing the right criteria to help form a business case. Each criterion must be measured. This allows you to compare proposals to select the best one to act on. Many criteria, such as cost and time, are simple to measure.

The flaw in many people's thinking is that they think some criteria cannot be measured. That is not true! Recall rule 2, that all measures are proxies. You can always find a proxy for any measure. Take the case of measuring judgment. Many smart people will tell you it can't be measured. Yet the following approach will show how it can be done:

- Be specific about what you need to measure. What areas of judgment are of most concern? If we are trying to justify changes to how we interview and hire staff, we want to focus on judgment when it comes to hiring decisions.
- Figure out what 'good looks like.' Try to identify what you want to see, not what you do not want to see. What does good judgment look like versus poor judgment, when it comes to hiring? Some simple options could include that good hires stay

---

[2] Available at *www.itgovernance.co.uk/shop/p-812-itil-2011-continual-service-improvement.aspx*.

longer. They earn higher ratings on their reviews. They are more likely to earn promotions.

- Pick a measure! Many people spend days, even weeks, trying to select the right measure. As the Law of Metrics states, such a beast does not exist. Review your options. Look for a relevant measure that is simple to gather and explain, credible to your stakeholders, and seems to correlate to what you want to know. In our example above, we might choose average review rating for hires because all employees get a review annually, so there is more data than for our other options.

Your measures form the foundation of a sound business case. Once your leaders decide to take action, you can then begin using the second reason for measures.

Measuring to direct (Do)

As you execute a plan, you use measurements to help guide action. Which project task should you tackle first? How many people need to work on the incidents that monitoring systems reported overnight? Which requests need to be escalated?

While this area is straightforward, there is one flaw to avoid: hard-to-read reports. Design reports and dashboards to make them easy to use.

- Show important items at the top. If your staff need to work requests in the order they are created, make sure the oldest ones are listed first.
- Highlight or bold items that have exceeded targets and require further action. Make them stand out so they are not missed.
- List only the details needed to complete the task. This keeps reports shorter and simpler.

These measures will ensure that things are done right. Yet how do you make sure that those actions are yielding intended outcomes? This drives the third reason for measurement.

Measuring to validate (Check)

As mentioned in *Chapter 2*, success must be defined by the customer. When we measure to validate, our intent is to show whether they got the intended value – or not. There are many pitfalls to avoid in this area:

- 'False' improvements. Remember rule 4. Once you measure something, there are incentives to make the measure look good. For example, you want to make sure enough staff are available to help customers at the start of the day. You start measuring when they clock in to work. After three weeks, the percentage of staff clocking in on time has gone up 50%. Time to celebrate? Maybe not! Are people clocking in, then going to breakfast? If so, your customers are getting little value from the change.

- Changing focus. Humans have an amazing ability to forget about pain. When you solve a problem, your customer's focus moves to other problems. If you make something faster, your customer may not appreciate it because they are now focused on costs.

- Adaptation. People get used to things quickly. If you improve the mean time to process a request from four hours to two hours, no one remembers that three hours used to be faster than normal. Now it is slow!

- Measures lose their 'shine.' Remember rules 3 and 5. As time passes, the flaws in any measure become more obvious. People often wonder why such a 'terrible' metric was used in the first place!

To minimize these drawbacks, use the following tactics:

- Clearly define the measure, assumptions, intended value, and other key information before the improvement is done. Also document other measures that were considered and why they were not used. This helps you maintain consistency and avoid change for the sake of change.

- Check the data frequently. Is it being created differently? What changes are affecting data quality and quantity?

- Carefully monitor where staff have incentives to 'game' the system. This is harder if your measures focus on getting more of what you want, instead of less of what you don't want. Even then, rule 4 still applies!

- Regularly publish current performance versus past performance, to remind people of how things were before the change. Do not shy away from marketing your successes when your team has earned them!

Even the best-planned projects can go astray. That then leads to the fourth and final reason for measurement.

Measuring to intervene (Act)

The goal of an intervention is to alter the course of events before it is too late. Modern life is full of complex systems. Even with good intent from all stakeholders, this sometimes results in sub-par outcomes. When you need to intervene, keep these thoughts in mind:

- Assume positive intent from everyone. It is easy for blame and finger pointing to begin when projects are not delivering intended results. Take every chance to assure people that they are not viewed as being bad, dumb, or lazy. If you ARE under those assumptions, stop! You're probably wrong. Even if you're not, since you can only observe behavior (*see Chapter 10*), you will never win an argument about someone's intent. So don't try.
- Focus attention on the desired outcomes. When folks get defensive, they are not thinking about results. They want to show compliance, so they can avoid being 'at fault.' Show them instead why better outcomes are needed. Describe the impact on customers. Better yet, have your customers describe the impact!
- Enlist help in solving the problem. The methods reviewed in *Chapter 14* are powerful in this situation. They are even more useful when you involve as many stakeholders as possible. This reduces the odds you will focus on the wrong problem.

Often, a small adjustment is all that is needed to put things on course. When larger changes are needed, it is best to create an updated justification. This brings the measurement circle back to its beginning.

It is easy to adopt bad habits when it comes to measurement. Political arguments often become more about 'winning' than about what is the right thing to do. We strive to reach a particular weight, or income level, or number of followers on social media. This is not effective in our personal lives (*see Chapter 1*), and it is harmful at work too.

The opportunity for you is that few managers use metrics well. You gain a huge advantage once you can apply these good practices. Combining this with the other skills reviewed in Part III, you can be confident that you are meeting your stewards' needs. There are great rewards for being a manager that can translate leader intent into results!

Action plan

- Identify the intent of measurement for your current reports and metrics
- Align your metrics and reports to your decision-making needs
- Teach these concepts to your team and peers

PART IV: EFFECTIVENESS WITH THE MARKETPLACE

'To give real service you must add something which cannot be bought or measured with money, and that is sincerity and integrity.' – Donald Adams

Customers are demanding. Their needs change constantly. Disruption is the norm. Today's leader must be nimble in thought and action. Service is survival.

CHAPTER 16: GET TO KNOW YOUR CUSTOMERS WITH DEMAND MANAGEMENT THINKING

'The demand for certainty is one which is natural to man, but is nevertheless an intellectual vice.' – Bertrand Russell

People are lousy forecasters. We are prone to error about the future of sporting events, the economy, or even the weather. We think we are right more often than we actually are. We ignore some facts and overreact to others. We overestimate change in the short run and underestimate it in the long run. We believe things will change, or stay the same, just because we want them to.

This is also true at work. Ask people what your organization needs to improve in and you will get all sorts of answers. Some will insist on cutting costs. Others will clamor for revising products and services. Still others will want to pivot to entirely new markets. Each camp can point to trends that support their position. What to do?

Understanding demand and what influences it is an essential skill for all business leaders, including those in IT. ITIL's demand management process can give you a useful approach for understanding the forces that drive demand and how they change. We will use a six step method to improve your ability to detect and respond to marketplace changes quickly.

Step 1: Identify sources of demand forecasting

Good forecasters start by understanding their current state. You must invest time and energy into finding good sources of information. These guidelines can help:

- Be aware of the world. While many news sources are a waste of time, you do need to have a general sense of what is going on around you. Whether you use newspapers, radio, TV, websites, or other methods, is up to you. The key is to find two to four sources that are trustworthy, relatively balanced as a whole, and have a broad focus. Try to use at least one local, one national, and one world source, to provide different perspectives on events. Scan them weekly at a minimum, and daily at best.

- Know what is going on in your industry. While reading the *Wall Street Journal* or *Fortune* is great, you can also use industry associations, blogs, and regular web searches, to keep up. Make friends in your industry at other companies. Attend conferences and webinars. Strive to connect with at least two sources each week.

- Don't forget your enterprise! Get to know folks in your forecasting, strategy, and/or planning areas. They can provide insight into the trends that are affecting your company. Another benefit is that they can often point you to additional resources for news and analysis that may be impossible through other means. Touch base with someone on your 'internal news' team at least biweekly.

- Refresh regularly. As mentioned in *Chapter 4*, these are streams of information. Get rid of sources that are not providing useful content. Try out new sources with different viewpoints. If nothing you see surprises you, you are doing it wrong!

Step 2: Analyze Patterns of Business Activity

Over time, you will begin to notice regular occurrences that affect your enterprise. These Patterns of Business Activity (PBAs) are crucial to understanding the rhythms of your business. For instance, a simple PBA could be that at noon on weekdays, a restaurant averages 100 to 200 customers during the lunch hour. Most of the patrons come in between 12:05 and 12:15. Each pattern can be described by changes in one or more of the following four factors:

1. Volume – How much demand is occurring?
2. Frequency – How regularly is the demand occurring?
3. Duration – How long does the demand occur?
4. Location – Where is the demand occurring?

Look for patterns in your daily business. For each PBA you identify, note which factor(s) are impacted, and how they are affected.

Step 3: Identify User Profiles

The patterns you identify are ultimately caused by the users of services. This could be a person, a group, a system, or another service. It is useful to create User Profiles (UPs) of the most common types of service users. For instance, a simple UP for our restaurant mentioned in step 2, would be a line worker who hates to cook and has strict limits on budget and time for lunch. Each UP can be described using these three familiar elements of a service:

1. Value – What utility and warranty does this UP want from our services?
2. Costs – How much time and money is this UP willing to invest in obtaining services?
3. Risks – Which potential negative outcomes are unacceptable to this UP, and which are tolerable, given the value and costs they want?

Identify the two to three UPs that generate the most business for your enterprise. For each UP, determine their value, cost, and risk profile.

Step 4: Manage activity-based demand

We can now start to put together a chain of causes and effects. Peter Senge describes a useful way of thinking about where demand comes from in *The Fifth Discipline*.

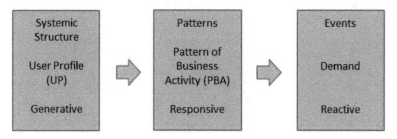

Figure 4: Demand cause and effect

With the work of steps 1-3, we can now start to understand how changes in the marketplace affect demand. In *figure 4* above, if a fancy steakhouse opens next door, it is unlikely to affect how often our line worker eats lunch at our restaurant. But a popular fast food chain is a different story!

For each UP identified in step 3, call out the types of changes most likely to occur. How would this affect their PBAs? What impact would this then have on demand? Look at situations where this has happened in the past, and see if your intuition matches the data. If not, examine why.

You can also use this approach in reverse. What recent changes in demand have occurred? What PBAs changed that led to these outcomes? What changes could have affected the related UPs? As you practice, you will start to notice more subtle factors and improve your judgment. Do not get cocky, though. Just when you think you understand demand, something new will occur!

Step 5: Adapt your service packages

An important benefit of understanding demand is being able to tailor your offerings. As discussed in *Chapter 12*, understanding what your leaders want is essential to making commitments you can keep. What they want is driven by the marketplace! When you understand what generates demand, you can start to adjust, even before your leaders do.

This is particularly important when the economy shifts. Let's say your enterprise's market is beginning to pick up. Your leaders will likely seek out your higher value services, even if they cost more and are riskier. If you notice this early, you can begin to shift your internal resources towards these services and away from your lower-value offerings.

You should also begin to tailor your business case proposals (*Chapter 11*). When your enterprise sees demand increasing, your leaders will focus on gaining revenue and market share. In a downturn, reducing costs is most critical. Sometimes a rejection does not mean 'never,' it means 'not right now.' Do not be afraid to bring up an old idea when the timing is better!

Step 6: Manage operational demand

Even with all of these practices in place, day-to-day demand will often shift. When this occurs, you, and your team, must adapt.

Here are some coping strategies to use for short-term variations in demand:

- Demand decreases
  o Invest in process improvement and problem solving. The idea is the old adage of 'saving for a rainy day.' Ideally, by the time demand increases, you will be able to deliver higher quality services for lower costs than you could before.
  o Train and develop your staff. Not only does it increase their engagement, you will increase consistency and quality of work. This also helps drive new ideas for improvement.
  o Innovate and experiment. Is someone on your team talking your ear off about a great idea? Have them create a test and try it out!
  o Help other areas of your enterprise. If you see your peers struggling, find areas where you can provide support. Not only does this help your business, it improves relationships and team cohesion.

- Demand increases
  o Reduce low-value services. It is easy to over-deliver low-value services when times are good. The challenge is that users become accustomed to higher service levels. Even when service exceeds agreements, reductions almost always cause negative perceptions. Be upfront and open with your customers when you make these changes. This helps you keep your credibility.
  o Ask for help from other areas. Do not be afraid to owe favors! Business is a team sport. This is yet another area where great relationships (*Chapter 6*) pay dividends.
  o Re-prioritize your team's work. You will be amazed what your people are working on. They may be working on things no longer needed. Perhaps it is a task they like to do, yet it has little or no value. Give them a 'get out of jail free' card on this work and ask them to stop. Tell them to refer anyone to you who complains. You can always pick a task back up if it is truly needed.
  o Bear down and do the work. This should be your last resort. Sometimes, a spike in demand requires a long night or weekend. Do not ask anyone to work longer hours unless you are willing to do them as well. If you do this more than once a quarter, that is too much! Revise your services or renegotiate instead!

As mentioned in *Chapter 13*, great leaders turn the uncertainty of the marketplace into certainty for their enterprise. The techniques described above can help you do this. There are few feelings more satisfying than seeing a trend, adjusting to it, and making a smooth correction while others panic. With practice, you too will become known as someone whose finger is on the pulse of your customers.

Another attribute needed to effectively serve your market is to understand its underlying needs. In *Chapter 17*, we will use the warranty practices of ITSM (Availability, Capacity, Continuity, and Security management) to define requirements.

Action plan

- Develop your sources to understand patterns of demand (PBAs)
- Identify the forces that affect users of your business' services
- Adjust your services as demand changes, to stay ahead of your leaders' needs

CHAPTER 17: IDENTIFYING UNDERLYING CUSTOMER NEEDS USING THE ITIL WARRANTY PROCESSES

'What the customer demands is last year's model, cheaper. To find out what the customer needs you have to understand what the customer is doing as well as he understands it. Then you build what he needs and you educate him to the fact that he needs it.' – Nick DeWolf

Have you ever been in a painful requirements meeting? The intent is often good – we need to know what customers want. But after 50-60 questions, many of which are about things the customer has never thought about, it becomes an ordeal. The worst part is that often the requirements are useless. They are not based on reality, but what we would like reality to be!

Managing requirements is a key element of business analysis. A good business analyst uses a variety of techniques to understand customer needs. A few examples include job shadowing, system analysis, prototyping, and interviews. The *Guide to the Business Analysis Body of Knowledge (BABOK)* is a helpful resource for how to use these tools, and when.

Even if you are not a business analyst, a core element of ITSM is that we need to understand customer needs. The use of PBAs and UPs in *Chapter 16* focuses on utility. Yet customers also have needs that support utility. How can we identify these needs? Often, customers do not even know these concerns exist (until they are not met!) The BABOK refers to these as non-functional requirements. ITIL's definition of warranty is a good starting point for defining these types of requirements.

Warranty – 'fit for use'

- Available when needed
- Enough capacity
- Maintains continuity
- Secure

In this chapter we will use this framework as a way to understand non-functional requirements. By using simple guidelines for each of these elements, you can ensure your service provides needed value, while reducing waste.

Availability

When services are unavailable, no value is being delivered. While simple, IT is notorious for not being able to share availability with customers in a way that makes sense to them. 'The network was up 99.93% last month'! Why should the customer care? How were they impacted?

It does not have to be this way! Whether you are talking about services from your team, your department, or your enterprise, a few simple guidelines can help.

- **Put a value on each of the services.** As mentioned in *Chapter 15*, there is no 'right' measure. The intent is to pick a value that seems fair to your stakeholders. Keep it simple to start. You want the discussions to focus on how to improve outcomes, not how to improve measures! Keep in mind that value does not always mean money. You may define value in terms of transactions lost, citizens not served, or pairs of shoes not made.

- **Define what counts as unavailable.** Again, the key is to gain agreement on a definition that seems fair. Most people start with global outages and local outages. Others count every incident. Neither approach is wrong – just be clear and open about your definition. Include a consensus on how to weigh different types of outages/incidents. For example, if there are five total locations, single location outages may count as 20% of a total outage.

- **Agree on timing.** Notice a theme here? Agreement is also needed on what time to use for the start and end of unavailability. Are there periods that should not count at all? Define them upfront, otherwise you will lose more time later debating the 'correct' approach.

With these rules in place, you can tell customers what unavailability cost them, in terms they understand. Here is a simple example. Suppose last week a service had critical outages (weighted 100%) that lasted two hours, and high outages (weighted 50%) that lasted eight hours. It is a 24x7 service worth $2.5 million per week.

- Total hours: 168
- Weighted critical outage hours: 2 * 100% = 2
- Weighted high outage hours: 8 * 50% = 4

- % of unavailability: (2 + 4) hours / 168 hours = ~3.57%
- Total value lost from unavailability: 3.57% * $2.5 million = $89,250

Telling your leaders that downtime cost them $89,250 is a lot more helpful than telling them you had 96.43% availability last week! You can now have useful discussions about how much to invest in improvements. It sharpens your ability to truly understand availability requirements. It also helps you talk to your staff about the value of what they do.

Capacity

Once upon a time, all computing capacity was expensive. Now, many consumers have more disk capacity in their home than most companies had 20 years ago. The impact is that capacity costs are no longer just about under-capacity. Overcapacity wastes energy, floor space, and attention better used in other areas. Yet utilization measures, such as percentage of disk space used, are not meaningful!

With this understanding, the measurements already defined for availability, and a few rules, you can estimate the capacity costs for services:

- **Identify which under-capacity issues to track.** These may include some items already called out earlier. Make sure everyone is clear on what counts and what does not, and how to weight them. You can then calculate the cost of under-capacity in the same way unavailability cost was calculated above.

- **Determine what buffers to use for components/ systems/services.** A *buffer* is additional capacity intended to handle spikes and overflows. This is not waste! The size of a buffer depends on many factors. How does demand vary? What does extra capacity cost? One example would be setting a rule that a server should always have at least ten percent of disk space free. Defining rules in this manner makes identifying capacity requirements much easier.

- **Assign a cost to each unit of capacity.** Yet again, don't worry about getting a precise, accurate figure. Select a value that seems reasonable to all stakeholders.

Suppose that a terabyte (TB) of disk space costs your enterprise $1,000. All storage arrays should have a ten percent buffer. You have a 250TB storage array, and it averaged 140TB of usage. Here is how you would compute the cost of unused capacity:

- Target capacity usage: 250TB – (10% * 250TB) = 225TB
- Amount of overcapacity: 225TB – 140TB = 85TB
- Cost of overcapacity: 85TB * ($1,000 per TB) = $85,000

Which measure is more meaningful to your audience: that $85,000 worth of capacity went unused, or that the disk array had 56% utilization? The first statement drives action. The second drives your non-technical customers crazy!

Continuity

As mentioned in *Chapter 14*, risks cannot be eliminated, only exchanged. Continuity planning is intended to reduce the risk that a disaster will put you out of business. It is a form of insurance. The issue is that most people do not like to pay for insurance until something happens and it is too late!

Help people see the value of continuity by making it real to them. Here are some tips that can help:

- **Find out what your customers worry about.** Natural disasters? Epidemics? Worker strikes? Recessions? You cannot prepare for everything, so focus on the items that keep them up at night.
- **Develop options to meet their concerns.** No matter what is the concern, there is a way to reduce its impact. Backup and/or redundant systems (perhaps from excess capacity!). Extra resources. Diversity of geography, industry, or investments. The analysis techniques in *Chapter 11* can help you analyze and compare ideas.
- **Gain agreement on continuity plans.** Review the options and select the ones that make sense for all stakeholders. Write them down.
- **Review them regularly with customers.** Worries change, and so do the options to address them. Adjust as needed. Another benefit of reviewing continuity plans regularly is that it reinforces their value with the customer. You do not want to

scare your customers. Just remind them of the peace of mind you provide.

Security

Insecurity is an awful feeling. Yet security is rarely thought about – until it is gone. This makes it difficult to assess its value. ISO27000 is the standard for how to manage information security. It provides a useful structure for discussing security requirements with customers.

- **Availability of information.** A useful system must be accessible. Security incidents that require systems to be taken offline are costly. The guidelines in the availability section above can be used to discuss costs with customers effectively.

- **Confidentiality of information.** What impact does it have on your customers if their information can be seen by others? For some customers, this is no big deal. For others, it is a catastrophe. Talk with your customers about who should have access to information. Is confidentiality a concern for your customers? If so, you should treat breaches like a disaster. Use the tips in the continuity section to address their needs.

- **Integrity of information.** In some areas, bad data is worse than no data. Consider Sharron, a stock trader. If she makes a large share purchase based on bad data, she could lose much more money than if no trade was made at all. It could even be a matter of life or death if we are talking about medical data! Ensure that information integrity requirements are considered in every process, every application, and every scenario. Consider logging all data changes. Establish data change controls. Perform regular system audits.

Translating customer needs into enterprise requirements is both a science and an art. You must balance being a pest with being out of touch. Fortunately, this is an area where 'in the land of the blind, the one eyed man is king.' A small amount of study and practice yields dividends. Better services. Improved relationships with customers. Credibility with your business partners.

Of course, none of this work helps if it is not used to build effective services. In *Chapter 18* we will explore how to use Service

Transition, Agile, and DevOps thinking to build, test, and deploy services that meet customer needs.

Action plan

- Define an agreed value for services used by your customers
- Document customer needs around availability, capacity, continuity, and security
- Come up with options to meet continuity and security concerns

CHAPTER 18: MANAGING PROJECTS USING RELEASE MANAGEMENT PRINCIPLES

'Everything flows, nothing stands still.' – Heraclitus

Have you ever been on the receiving end of a really bad roll out? Perhaps you got an email on a Friday afternoon that a new application was going live Monday. Training consisted of a link to an FAQ document that you did not have permission to view. Maybe your team was even listed as supporting the new system!

Moving systems from development to production is difficult for most IT organizations. Project teams are trying to complete their work on time and on budget. Operations teams are trying to keep systems up and provide useful, timely support. The conflicts result in lousy systems, ill will, and unhappy customers.

Today, there are many approaches for making the transition faster and safer. Traditional Systems Development Life Cycle (SDLC) work flows focus on documenting formal requirements and designing a system all at once that meets those needs. Agile and DevOps approaches focus on shortening cycle times, with increased customer involvement. Project management approaches, such as PMBOK and PRINCE2 help manage the scope of work.

ITIL's release and deployment management process can be used in conjunction with any of these ideas. In this chapter we will show how the release and deployment process can help you minimize waste and maximize value when you are running a project.

Step 1: Plan for the release

Good release planning starts with knowing what success means. High-quality technology is not enough. It is more than deploying without errors. You must also be able to fully operate the system and get results. Keep these ideas in mind:

- Who is sponsoring your release? What do they expect? How will decisions be made? What counts as success? Get this in writing!
- Size the work appropriately. Trying to do new things in large batches is a recipe for failure! A key principle of Agile and DevOps is to rapidly deliver value and get feedback. How

certain are you that you can deliver what is needed? If you have prior success in the work you are doing, larger blocks of work are fine. If you are doing something unfamiliar, figure out the smallest chunk of value you can deliver the fastest. Eric Ries' *The Lean Startup* calls this the 'Minimal Viable Product (MVP).' By focusing on the MVP, you reduce uncertainty, and give people something useful faster.

- Set guardrails upfront on costs, time, and quality. It is easy to focus on completing tasks instead of delivering value. If you do not set limits in advance, you could fall prey to the sunk cost fallacy. You tell yourself 'we are almost there' over and over. At some point, cost overruns and poor systems exceed the expected benefits. If you reach that point, stop! Figure out your thresholds, write them down, and communicate them to your leaders. If you can't figure out how to do this, reduce the scope of work until you can.

- Determine who else needs to be involved, and when. For every area you identify, talk with them upfront about their needs. Are there templates, prior plans, or successful releases you can learn from? This allows you to avoid headaches later on.

- Define your testing approach. A large part of your quality guardrails should focus on testing. ITIL's Service Validation and Testing (SV&T) process is a useful starting point to figure out what tests are needed. These areas are especially important:

  o Outcome tests: Does the release provide the needed results? For instance, can you reduce costs like you expected? This is the most important test of all!

  o User acceptance tests: Can people find what they need? Can they easily get help? Do users want to do things differently than intended? An unused or bypassed system is as bad as a broken one.

  o Utility and warranty tests: Is the release producing the performance needed? Is there enough capacity? Is it secure? Does it meet requirements (as discussed in *Chapter 17*)? Meeting commitments is essential.

  o Deployment and installation tests: How quickly can you install the release? How well can you back out if there are issues? How disruptive is a deployment? How much variation is there between documented procedures and what actually has to be done? Do not assume that everything will go as planned.

o Component tests: Are any subsystems error-prone? Do they work well together? Does each piece deliver the outputs needed?

- Make sure you can run what you build. Everything breaks and wears out. Who will provide support? What support documentation and tools do they need? Do they know how to fix incidents? What monitoring is needed to avoid outages? Who needs to be involved if there is a problem?

- Plan for the whole lifecycle. How will you maintain the system? How hard is it to upgrade and enhance? What can you do if a component is no longer available and/or supported? How is the configuration documented?

Step 2: Prepare for build, test, and deployment

Before creating the release, make sure you have the resources and capabilities needed to deliver. There are many elements that can cause failure if ignored:

- Do your staff need training, in order to build the release?
- Can you get the money, technology, people, and/or information required, when needed?
- Will test environments, and staff, be available when needed?
- Is the amount of change planned at any given time more than the enterprise can handle?
- Are there other projects affecting this space that could cause conflict?
- What staffing changes are needed by support and maintenance teams, to operate the system once deployed?
- How will needed documentation be created as work is performed?
- Do you have leadership support for any needed changes to processes, procedures, or metrics?
- Will you require any new contracts or agreements to obtain needed resources?
- How long will the project team support the release once it is deployed?

Remember that you do not have to figure everything out by yourself. Review lessons learned from other projects. Do not be afraid to ask for input. Even if you cannot meet a need, it is better to be aware of it, so you can address it early.

Step 3: Build and test

Creating a release is both an art and a science. You acquire raw materials and combine them to create something new. There is no such thing as a 'turn-key' solution. Even if you are buying a product, you must create new ways for your staff to use it.

Everyone must have a clear picture of who is doing what by when (as Manager Tools phrases it). Do not confuse this with certainty! Clear milestones are even more important when you are doing something new. You must be able to quickly identify when an assumption is untrue. Shorter deadlines lower risk.

Get updates from project team members regularly. Whether you use a daily standup meeting, a Kanban board, formal project status meetings, or something else, depends on your approach and work culture. Part of your job is to encourage communication. Provide frequent feedback to your team members (*Chapter 10*) about sharing with others.

Every milestone should include some kind of internal test. Avoid having people test their own stuff. This can be as simple as having someone else look at the result. You may also have systems that can check code integrity, logic, etc. Good testing builds confidence and reduces the odds of failure.

Step 4: Test and pilot

Once you have created the release, you will want to perform many of the tests described in step 1. Use your enterprise's formal test approach, if it has one. If not, ITIL's SV&T process recommends a six part method for successful testing:

1. *Plan and design tests.* For each test identified in step 1, define how to carry it out. Who will manage the test? Who decides if it was successful? What criteria will they use? Who else will participate? How much time is needed? What systems are available?

2. *Verify test plans.* Just like with component tests, you want another set of eyes on test plans. Get input on gaps and

concerns, and make changes as needed. While you cannot test everything, you do not want to miss something obvious.

3. *Prepare the test environment.* Some tests require a lot of setup time and coordination. Is everyone available at the needed time? Are support documents for the test ready for use? What differences exist between the test and production environment? Make sure you can actually test what you think you are testing. Try not to assume things you cannot validate. Bad testing is worse than no testing!

4. *Perform tests.* Your tests will find errors. Document and research them. Correct them if you can. Sometimes it is better to accept an error than to try to fix it. This depends on several factors. How long will the fixes take? How many things depend on the part being updated? How easy is it to redo prior tests? How much pain does the error cause? How much appetite is there for risk?

5. *Evaluate exit criteria and report.* Once testing is complete, share what you learned with stakeholders. Are you getting the intended outcomes? What was the user experience like? How much demand can be handled? Evaluate the results against the thresholds you defined in step 1. If the project is not delivering what is needed, ask for a decision on what to do next from your sponsor.

6. *Close and clean up the test.* Announce next steps and return resources as needed. Ask for feedback. Take a few minutes to write down what you learned. What worked well? What needs to be improved? What surprised you?

Always aim to pilot your release when there is a high risk of failure. Try it with one person or team. Divert one percent of requests to the new system. Install it in a single location. Some things cannot be learned until people use the system to get things done.

Set clear guidelines around when you will pilot. How do you remove it when finished? What results warrant leaving the pilot in place? How do you end it quickly if it fails?

Step 5: Plan and prepare deployment

While some deployment planning can be done upfront, much of it must wait until the release is built. Make sure the following items are considered before making changes:

- Training
  - o Are documentation, simulations, videos, etc., ready for users, support staff, installers, and maintenance teams?
  - o Who is conducting the training? Are they prepared?
  - o Have training sessions been scheduled? What is in place for people that miss those sessions?
  - o How will new staff be trained going forward? Who will update materials as your enterprise learns and grows?
- Suppliers
  - o Are contracts changing? If so, how can you time those changes to minimize risk?
  - o Are suppliers ready for any changes in demand from your enterprise?
  - o Did you renegotiate service levels? If so, is everyone aware of the new agreements?
  - o How are licenses, warranties, and other assets, being tracked?
  - o What procedures are needed to make sure necessary equipment is in place when needed?
- Installation/removal
  - o Have installation procedures been updated to reflect results from testing?
  - o Do installers have the access needed to do the work?
  - o Do you have agreements on when you can begin installing the release, and when you must be done?
  - o When must a decision be made on whether to back out of an installation, so it can be completed in time? Who decides?
  - o Who will help if installers encounter incidents they cannot fix?
  - o How will problems be identified, tracked, and reported?
  - o What old equipment, documents, and/or systems, need to be retired? How will these items be redeployed, removed, archived, and/or disposed?
- Status
  - o Where will progress be tracked?
  - o How will everyone affected by the release be notified of activities they care about?
  - o Who needs to be updated if schedules change?
  - o What confirmation is needed that key messages have been received?

While this is a long list, many small deployments can be summarized on one page. This is another reason to keep your release size small.

Step 6: Perform transfer, deployment, and retirement

This step is similar to step 3. Manage to key milestones. Make sure installers are clear on their assignments and deadlines. Provide guidance on when to escalate issues and concerns. Check in regularly on progress. Go see what is really happening, as well as what is reported!

It is inevitable that unexpected situations will occur. When they do, focus on problem solving, not blaming. Use the techniques in *Chapter 14* to determine causes and ways to fix them. Assume positive intent from everyone involved until you have convincing evidence otherwise. Encourage openness. Celebrate progress!

Step 7: Verify deployment

Touch base with your stakeholders as deployment occurs. Are you getting the intended results? What seems to be going well? What issues are they facing? Do people feel it is successful? Document their input and ask for ideas on how to address their concerns. Many times, a small adjustment can make a big difference.

Step 8: Early Life Support (ELS)

Beginnings are delicate times. A smooth project does not guarantee an issue-free transition. Have your release team help with initial support. This provides several benefits:

- Reduces the odds that issues will overwhelm operations and reduce support for other areas
- Improves development team understanding of operations
- Increases operational team knowledge of the new system
- Faster correction of documentation issues
- Builds stronger relationships between development and operational teams
- Shortens time to identify problems and useful enhancements

As mentioned in step 2, you should define criteria for how long ELS will last. A good approach is to define criteria based on changes to incident and problem volume. For example, ELS could be set to end once incident volume is at, or below, pre-release levels. This rewards release teams that deliver with high quality.

Step 9: Review and close

Once installation is complete, your work is not over. Make sure you have achieved the intended results. Did sales go up? Are costs now less? If not, why?

Regardless of the outcomes, you should always capture what was learned from the project. Get input from others when possible.

- Were there unexpected obstacles?
- How good were your estimates?
- What risks were you able to avoid?
- Which relationships got stronger?
- Who did good work and could be a future fit for your staff?
- What skills do you need to improve?
- What feedback can you give each team member that will help them in the future?

Do not forget to celebrate success! Invite senior leaders to thank the team for their work. Give them specific details on which team member did what. This allows your leaders to know who did well, and your team members to get meaningful appreciation. Few people do this, and it is a simple way to end things positively.

You must become competent at project management to be an effective manager. It is not complex, yet it is not easy. You must track details, influence others, and communicate clearly at all levels. Volunteer to lead projects when you get the chance. Even a two-week effort can benefit from these ideas.

Good planning reduces surprises, yet it cannot eliminate all of them. When the unexpected happens, you must be able to adapt to the situation and provide what is needed. In *Chapter 19* we will review ways that ITIL's incident management process can help us deal with disruption.

Action plan

- Learn the basics of managing projects/releases
- Practice planning and executing projects
- Learn from your triumphs and mistakes

CHAPTER 19: HELPING YOUR CUSTOMERS WHEN THINGS GO WRONG WITH GOOD INCIDENT MANAGEMENT

'High expectations are the key to everything.' – Sam Walton

Think about the last time you had an issue with a product or service. Companies spend billions of dollars every year trying to win back customers. Most of them leave for one simple reason. *They did not feel valued.*

Complaints and issues are inevitable. Handling them well is not. Yet doing so is not hard. The key is to take ownership. The person is not just <u>a</u> customer, they are <u>your</u> customer. <u>You</u> are going to make sure they get what they need, or as close as <u>you</u> can provide.

There are two parts to every complaint: the issue and how your customer feels about it. You can use ITIL's incident management process and good customer service techniques to address both parts. The benefit is better understanding of your customers, and stronger relationships with them. This guidance can help whether you manage a service desk, or just need to help a co-worker.

Step 1: Identify the incident

Good identification starts with listening. Let people tell you about their issue. Do not try to guess, problem solve, or hurry them along. Ask them clarifying questions – in their terms. What were they trying to do? What is not happening because of the issue? How often does this happen? Restate their complaint, and ask them if it is accurate.

Keep in mind that even if you deal with this complaint 1,000 times a week, your customer does not. Don't sigh, don't chuckle, and don't roll your eyes. After all, you may be wrong!

Express empathy for their situation. Even if their issue is self-inflicted, they are still unable to do what they want. Even a simple 'That must be frustrating' or 'That stinks,' can go a long way. Help your customer understand that you want to work with them, not against them.

Step 2: Record, categorize, and prioritize the incident

Once you and your customer are on the same page, you can get the other information you need to serve them. Trying to do this first rarely works well. It sends the message 'my needs are more important than your needs.' That is not the feeling you want them to have!

Document the information so it is available to others when needed. Few things alienate customers faster than asking them to repeat themselves. Use other knowledge sources to reduce the number of questions you need to ask.

Categorize the incident based on either the service, or the component, they are trying to use. This keeps the focus on value, which is what matters to the customer. It also helps you figure out the priority to assign. Keep your priority range simple. Think 'now, next, or normal':

- Interrupt a lower priority task and do it *now*
- Put it on top of the stack to be done *next*
- Put it on the bottom of the stack to be done *normally*

In all cases, <u>set clear expectations with your customer on what is being done</u>. Tell them when they should expect resolution. If you don't know, tell them when you will update them on progress. Always make sure your customers know when, and how, they will be updated. This reduces their anxiety, and the likelihood that they will complain to others and/or escalate.

Step 3: Initially diagnose the incident

Your incident types most likely follow the 80/20 rule: most of the complaints you get are related to a few types of issues. ITIL recommends defining models for your most common types of incidents. It need not be complex – just a few simple rules for each service, or component, will suffice:

- What information do we need to gather to understand the current state? How can we get it?
- Are there possible fixes that often work, are low risk, and can be done quickly?
- Is there a work flow we should follow for this type of incident?
- What indicates that the incident cannot be fixed quickly?

- How can we best determine where to escalate for help?
- Where can we get the data needed to restore service?

Focus on what you *can* do for your customer. Use phrases like 'the easiest way to ...' and 'the simplest way to ...' in order to share possible solutions. If you can't fix it right away, is there a substitute they can use until the incident is resolved? If you can't fix the issue, give them a way to cope.

Step 4: Escalate the incident

Identify if the incident is within the scope of your team to investigate, or if you need help. Good escalations are simple, yet not easy. Poorly handled escalations kill relationships. It is tempting to pat your customer on the back, give them a phone number, and wish them luck. Do not do this! Maintain ownership of the incident for the customer at all times.

Use these tips for effective escalations:

- Make sure whoever you escalate to receives and acknowledges your escalation.
- Get an estimate from your escalation point on when to expect a fix. If they don't know when it will be fixed, at least have them commit to when they will update you.
- Provide all needed info for further research. When an escalation area has to directly contact your customer for more information, a bad experience is often the result.
- For your most frequent types of escalations, document what information you need to provide. This improves consistency and makes others more willing, and able, to help.
- Give your escalation point your contact info, and who to contact if you are unavailable.

Update your leadership if they could be asked about the incident. Communicate the key details they need to know. What is the customer impact? Who is working on the incident? When was the customer last updated? When do you estimate service will be restored? When will you update them again?

Keep your customer informed of progress, not politics. They do not care how poorly other people are doing, nor that the issue is not your fault. Focus on new workaround options, when a fix is expected, and when they will be updated. Your customer wants to know that you are competent, and that you care.

Step 5: Investigate the incident

Your ability to troubleshoot is a valuable skill. While models can help with the majority of incidents, some situations will catch you off-guard. The problem guidance in *Chapter 14* is useful for difficult incidents. You can also use the scientific method, as follows:

- Start with your incident statement and information already gathered.
- Create a hypothesis on the cause of the incident. If you're stuck, try to identify things that have changed. Ask your customer if they noticed anything odd. Check for change schedules, announcements, or even news headlines. Consult knowledge bases, other people, and web search engines.
- Test your hypothesis. If it could be one of several items, try to test in a way that you can eliminate multiple possible causes at once. For example, if there are six possible failure points, try to test three of them at once. This allows you to narrow down the list of suspects faster.
- Review the results of your test and update your hypothesis, until it is confirmed by your test.

Make sure that anything you learn that can be useful in the future is captured in your SKMS (*Chapter 3*).

Step 6: Recover service and resolve the incident

Identifying the cause does not mean your work is over! You must still figure out the best way to restore service. If you have an approved procedure, use that. If not, consider these points before taking action:

- Am I changing something that others need to know about? Will what you plan to do make diagrams, procedures, or system data incorrect? Use good change procedures (*Chapter 8*) to ensure records are up to date.
- What is the risk if something goes wrong? It is easy to make a tiny issue a big one with a botched fix. If you are doing

something new, review your plan with someone else. They will often see gaps that could cause pain.

- Is it best to make the fix now, or during a slower period? If there is a high impact, it is often worth the risk to put the fix in right away. Yet often it makes sense to wait.

- All of these ideas apply to escalations, too. Ask your escalation point to notify you *before* they try to fix the incident. This allows you to prepare as needed.

- Involve your customer before attempting to recover if guidelines or risks are unclear. They ultimately should decide whether the potential impact of a failed fix is acceptable.

Step 7: Verify restoration and close the incident

Do not assume your fix worked. *Always* confirm with the customer that their service is back to normal. This not only avoids premature closure, it also allows you to end on a positive note. Capture feedback on how the incident was handled, for future improvements.

Update your records. What you thought at the start of the incident is often different from what you know at the end. This is valuable information. You may even identify areas where procedures, training, and tools, can be improved for future incidents.

Incidents can be stressful and unpredictable. Using a consistent approach allows you to focus on the incident and the customer, instead of on logistics. It helps you gain a reputation as someone who is calm, helpful, and professional, even in difficult situations. Your customers, leaders, and staff, will benefit, and you will have greater respect and influence.

While good incident management helps us with acute issues, more work is needed to address chronic gaps. In *Chapter 20* we will look at how assessments can help you identify areas for improvement that will deliver the most value for your customers.

Action plan

- Define incident models for the most common issues you handle

- Practice listening, understanding, empathy, and communication, when issues are brought to your attention
- Work on troubleshooting skills and techniques

CHAPTER 20: ASSESSING PERFORMANCE TO PREPARE FOR IMPROVEMENT

'If you don't set a baseline standard for what you'll accept in life, you'll find it's easy to slip into behaviors and attitudes, or a quality of life, that's far below what you deserve.'
– Tony Robbins

History shows us that success often stifles change. It is easy to assume past victories mean future choices will also lead to success. While you are celebrating, your competitors are working. You ignore trends and laugh at new offerings that are cheap and brittle. The laughter turns to panic and fear as the market embraces the innovation. Too often, the end result is another example of complacency leading to failure.

One cure for this condition is to regularly assess your organization's current state. As you identify gaps, you can work with your leaders to prioritize and fix them. The result is less waste and more value for your customers.

ITIL recommends using a best practice framework, such as COBIT, for conducting assessments. In this chapter we will use the seven enablers of COBIT 5 that we briefly touched on in *Chapter 14*. This ensures we look at all the elements that affect results. It can be used as a basis for assessing your team, department, or enterprise. We will examine each enabler from four vantage points:

1. Key stakeholders – everyone that is interested in that enabler and its results
2. Goals – the outcomes that the enabler is intended to deliver
3. Lifecycle – the plan, design, creation, use, and improvement of the enabler
4. Good practices – how work is performed, with references to other sources for more depth

The chapter will conclude with a four step approach to conducting assessments.

Enabler 1: Services, infrastructure, and applications

It is important to start with your services because they are how customers receive value. If customers do not want your services, none of the other enablers will keep you in business!

- Key stakeholders
  - o Customers of your services
  - o Staff that provide the components of your services
  - o Suppliers of the inputs to your services
- Goals
  - o Provide utility and warranty
  - o Minimize risks
  - o Optimize resources
- Lifecycle (ITIL service lifecycle)
  - o Strategy
  - o Design
  - o Transition
  - o Operation
  - o Improvement
- Good practices
  - o ITSM guidance, such as ITIL and ISO20000
  - o Service guidance, such as OBASHI and BiSL
  - o Architecture approaches, such as TOGAF® and the Zachman Framework

Enabler 2: Principles, policies, and frameworks

This enabler focuses on how you set rules and carry out decisions. Principles are the vision, mission, and values that define what matters most. Policies provide guidance on how to make decisions to align with principles. Frameworks provide detailed support and show how all the elements fit together.

- Stakeholders
  - o The board and executive leaders that define the direction
  - o Managers and staff that must comply
  - o Governments and regulators that define laws and industry rules
  - o Customers and suppliers affected by how decisions are carried out
- Goals
  - o Principles

- ♦ Clarify what matters
- ♦ Focus on long-term perspectives
  - o Policies
    - ♦ Effectively deliver intended results
    - ♦ Efficiently use resources
    - ♦ Demonstrate logic and reasoning
    - ♦ Be accessible to those that need them
  - o Frameworks
    - ♦ Cover all areas involved
    - ♦ Reflect current state of knowledge
    - ♦ Flexible enough to adapt to your needs
- Lifecycle (based on Bain & Company's RAPID model)
  - o Identify need for rule/decision
  - o Obtain input
  - o Develop recommendation
  - o Gain agreement from stakeholders
  - o Decide on choice and plan of action
  - o Perform the decision
- Good practices
  - o Governance guidance, such as ISO38500
  - o Decision tools, such as Bain & Company's RAPID model

Enabler 3: People, skills, and competencies

Everything starts with people. They are a resource and capability that are at the heart of every enabler.

- Stakeholders
  - o Enterprise leaders – define what skills and competencies are needed
  - o Training providers – internal and external developers of skills and competencies
  - o Users – apply skills and competencies to tasks
- Goals
  - o Develop appropriate mastery of skills and competencies
  - o Ensure succession plans are in place for core competencies
  - o Attract and retain staff with sufficient talent to deliver to organizational needs
- Lifecycle (four stages of competence)
  - o Unconscious incompetence – don't know what you don't know
  - o Conscious incompetence – aware of need and desire to learn

- o Conscious competence – able to perform the skill when focused
- o Unconscious competence – performs as needed, with little awareness of how it is done
- Good practices
  - o Skills Framework for the Information Age (SFIA)

Enabler 4: Organizational structures

Role power is a fundamental part of human existence. Organizational structures define decision rights and boundaries.

- Stakeholders
  - o Individual contributors
  - o Managers
  - o Executive leaders
  - o External people affected by decisions
- Goals
  - o Make decisions that deliver value, minimize risks, and optimize resource use in the short and long term
  - o Ensure decisions consider relevant facts and knowledge
  - o Decide quickly enough to take advantage of opportunities
- Lifecycle (from ITIL service strategy organizational structures)
  - o Network – informal and ad hoc
  - o Directive – centralized hierarchy
  - o Delegation – limited autonomy
  - o Coordination – formalized process
  - o Collaboration – matrix structure
- Good practices
  - o Industry-specific operating models, such as eTOM
  - o ITIL service strategy

Enabler 5: Culture, ethics, and behavior

Rewards and punishments drive behavior and culture. Incentives can be official or unofficial. They are often unspoken and unseen by those in the enterprise, like the air we breathe.

- Stakeholders
  - o Everyone internal to the enterprise
  - o External regulators
  - o Communities and societies that host the enterprise

- Goals
  - o Comply with organizational ethics, as defined by the enterprise's principles
  - o Ensure incentives align to enterprise objectives
  - o Encourage behaviors that lead to desired outcomes
    - ◆ Risk management
    - ◆ Adherence to process
    - ◆ Learning from mistakes
- Lifecycle (based on Tuckman's stages of group development)
  - o Creation of group (forming)
  - o Conflict of viewpoints (storming)
  - o Formation of accepted behaviors (norming)
  - o Anchored beliefs (performing)
  - o Cultural change (reforming)
- Good practices
  - o Organizational models, such as Deal and Kennedy, Schein, etc.
  - o Organizational change models, such as Kotter, Conner, etc.

Enabler 6: Processes

Process maturity is essential to consistent delivery of value. While it is often overemphasized compared to other enablers, it should not be ignored.

- Stakeholders
  - o Suppliers – those that provide inputs into the process
  - o Participants – those that own, manage, and perform the process
  - o Customers – those that receive outputs from the process
- Goals
  - o Effectively deliver desired outcomes
  - o Efficiently use resources
  - o Execute well, with the proper quality
  - o Comply with policies and standards
- Lifecycle (ISO15504 maturity model)
  - o Incomplete – not fully executed
  - o Performed – ad hoc
  - o Managed – some structure
  - o Established – consistently executed
  - o Predictable – delivers to defined objectives
  - o Optimizing – aligned to organizational strategy

- Good practices
  - o Process frameworks, such as ITIL and COBIT 5: Enabling Processes
  - o Process maturity models, such as CMMI-SVC and ISO15504

Enabler 7: Information

Facts and perceptions are the inputs to decisions. Bad information is worse than no information!

- Stakeholders
  - o Producers of information – processes, systems, etc.
  - o Custodians of information – databases, logs, etc.
  - o Consumers of information – monitoring tools, decision makers, etc.
- Goals
  - o Conforms to true values – accurate, believable, etc.
  - o Useful – relevant, current, concise, etc.
  - o Secure – availability, confidentiality, integrity
- Lifecycle (based on COBIT 5: Enabling Information model)
  - o Define data models
  - o Design data structures
  - o Create and acquire data
  - o Use data (DIKW – *see Chapter 3 for more guidance*)
  - o Monitor/update data practices
  - o Dispose data
- Good practices
  - o COBIT 5: Enabling Information
  - o Data Management Associate Data Management Body of Knowledge (DAMA-DMBOK)

Assessment approach

That is an intimidating list! Don't worry, you only need a small subset of this list to get started. Use the following four-step approach to conduct an assessment.

Step 1: Define the baseline

Assessments require a basis for comparison. This can be a subset of the above list, or an ISO standard. Zeithaml, Berry, and

Parasuraman's Service Gap model (described in the ITIL CSI book[3]) is useful if you want a holistic lifecycle approach. You can also use a benchmark from another enterprise. Whatever you use, be specific. Use these questions if you do not have an obvious starting point.

- What does success mean?
- How would you tell if your enterprise were successful or not?
- Who is the leader in your field, and what do they do?

Define the scope of your assessment. Is process maturity really what people care about? If the focus is on results, make sure all the enablers above are looked at. After all, they can each cause poor outcomes!

Once you have a proposed list, review it with the key stakeholders. Include their input. Get sign-off from your leaders and publish the criteria upfront. This reduces the temptation to change the criteria to meet results. Remember, the point of an assessment is not to look good. It is to find ways to get better!

Step 2: Capture the current state

For each item in your list, gather data on the current state of that item. Different items require different methods. Query systems. Interview stakeholders. Observe work and take notes. Send out surveys. Review documents.

Strive to be accurate, yet do not let that stop you. If people are afraid to share information, ask if anonymous feedback can be used. If data is wrong, ask why, and note it. If all else fails, note that the item cannot be assessed and propose ways to make it possible the next time.

Be sure to get feedback on your findings. If stakeholders disagree with your statements, ask them for comments and include them. This provides a fuller picture and helps people focus on solving problems instead of placing blame.

---

[3] Available at *www.itgovernance.co.uk/shop/p-812-itil-2011-continual-service-improvement.aspx*.

Step 3: Review and prioritize the gaps

Once you have your baseline and current state, identify the differences. Rank them based on how much value you would get from closing the gap. You can also look for dependencies that indicate what needs to be fixed first.

Continue to involve your stakeholders. Show them your ranked list and ask them what they think. Adjust where it makes sense. Use the negotiation skills discussed in *Chapter 12* to drive consensus.

Once your list is finalized, publish the results, and review with your leaders. Assessments are a persuasive tool for getting support for new projects and initiatives. Do not put it on a shelf and go back to work. An assessment that does not drive action is worthless!

Step 4: Identify lessons learned and schedule the next assessment

You are not done once you publish your assessment. Take the time to reflect on what worked well, and what did not. Update your assessment plan while events are still fresh in your mind. Ask for candid feedback from people you trust, and adjust.

Assessments become more valuable when they are repeated. You can not only compare to the standard, you can compare to your prior state. Make sure to schedule the next assessment while this one is still fresh in your mind. Block off time on your calendar. Set reminders. It is much easier to schedule time now than in a year!

Assessments are another example of something that is simple, yet not easy. They are quite versatile. You can even assess yourself, as shown in *Chapter 1* and *5*. The key is to call out expectations and be frank about reality.

You now have a comprehensive set of tools you can use to address any situation. The ideas can be applied in many areas beyond those discussed. Yet reading about them is not enough – you must take action. Be bold, strive to be great, and learn from your mistakes. Best of luck on achieving success, however you define it!

Action plan

- Practice assessing situations holistically, using the seven enablers
- Volunteer to lead an assessment effort in your team or department
- Involve staff throughout assessments to increase buy-in and commitment

EPILOGUE

'How long are you going to wait before you demand the best for yourself and in no instance bypass the discriminations of reason'? – Epictetus

This book focuses on management, yet the ideas can be applied to any space. On the surface, it is not clear why that should be true. After all, ITIL has only been around since the 1980s. Even more so, how could a set of books about keeping IT systems up possibly relate to anything else?

While ITSM may be relatively new, the ideas behind it are not. Consider the four primary threads that fed each part of this book:

1. We must focus on what is important (Part I)
2. Relationships matter (Part II)
3. We cannot control results, we can only influence them (Part III)
4. We receive value only when we provide value to others through service (Part IV)

Add in the fact that everything has a lifecycle. All five of these ideas are central to ITSM. Yet the combination yields a philosophy that can be applied anywhere. That may seem grand considering most people first encounter ITSM while working on technology. Yet that makes it no less so. Many people (the author included) find that they see service management everywhere – at the store, in the home, and in every aspect of their lives.

How would you behave if you adopted these ideas? You would waste less time on things that ultimately do not matter. You would consider the effects of your behaviors on those you are connected to. You would strive to do your best, while accepting that you will not always get exactly what you want. You would help others when you could. Lastly, you would treat each moment as meaningful because nothing lasts forever, yet good things are coming all the time.

The secret is that ITSM is just another way of saying that everything is connected and interdependent. This is also the conclusion drawn from studying ecology, sociology, religion, networks, or most other fields. The lesson? We are the cause of our own problems – yet we can also be part of the solution!

Roger K. Williams
May 1, 2014

FURTHER READING AND LEARNING

Books/Publications

- *Architecture Patterns for IT* by Charles Betz
- *ITIL* by AXELOS
- *COBIT 5* by ISACA
- *The Effective Executive* by Peter Drucker
- *The Fifth Discipline* by Peter Senge
- *How to Measure Anything* by Douglas Hubbard
- *Flawless Consulting* by Peter Block
- *The Power of Pull* by John Hagel III, John Seely Brown, and Lang Davison
- *Run Grow Transform* by Steve Bell
- *The Lean Startup* by Eric Ries
- *The Org* by Ray Fisman and Tim Sullivan
- *The Art of War* by Sun Tzu
- *The Seven Habits of Highly Effective People* by Stephen Covey
- *The Five Dysfunctions of a Team* by Patrick Lencioni
- *Hire With Your Head* by Lou Adler
- *The One Minute Manager* by Ken Blanchard
- *Drive* by Daniel Pink
- *The Goal* by Eli Goldratt

Web

- Manager Tools (*www.manager-tools.com*)
- Rands in Repose (*www.randsinrepose.com*)

ITG RESOURCES

IT Governance Ltd sources, creates and delivers products and services to meet the real-world, evolving IT governance needs of today's organisations, directors, managers and practitioners.

The ITG website (*www.itgovernance.co.uk*) is the international one-stop-shop for corporate and IT governance information, advice, guidance, books, tools, training and consultancy. On the website you will find the following pages related to IT service management and the subject matter of this book:

www.itgovernance.co.uk/itsm.aspx

www.itgovernance.co.uk/iso20000.aspx

www.itgovernance.co.uk/itil.aspx.

Publishing Services

IT Governance Publishing (ITGP) is the world's leading IT-GRC publishing imprint that is wholly owned by IT Governance Ltd.

With books and tools covering all IT governance, risk and compliance frameworks, we are the publisher of choice for authors and distributors alike, producing unique and practical publications of the highest quality, in the latest formats available, which readers will find invaluable.

www.itgovernancepublishing.co.uk is the website dedicated to ITGP. Other titles published by ITGP that may be of interest include:

- The ITSM Thought Leadership Series

  www.itgovernance.co.uk/shop/p-1398.aspx

- The Daniel McLean ITSM Fiction Series

  www.itgovernance.co.uk/shop/p-1526.aspx

- ITIL Lifecycle Essentials

  www.itgovernance.co.uk/shop/p-1285.aspx.

We also offer a range of off-the-shelf toolkits that give comprehensive, customisable documents to help users create the specific documentation they need to properly implement a management system or standard. Written by experienced practitioners and based on the latest best practice, ITGP toolkits can save months of work for organisations working towards compliance with a given standard.

Toolkits that may be of interest include:

- ITSM, ITIL® & ISO/IEC 20000 Implementation Toolkit

  www.itgovernance.co.uk/shop/p-872.aspx

- IT Governance Control Framework Implementation Toolkit

  www.itgovernance.co.uk/shop/p-1305.aspx

- ISO/IEC 20000 Documentation Toolkit

  www.itgovernance.co.uk/shop/p-632.aspx.

Books and tools published by IT Governance Publishing (ITGP) are available from all business booksellers and the following websites:

www.itgovernance.eu   *www.itgovernanceusa.com*

www.itgovernance.in   *www.itgovernancesa.co.za*

www.itgovernance.asia.

Training Services

IT Governance offers an extensive portfolio of training courses designed to educate information security, IT governance, risk management and compliance professionals. Our classroom and online training programmes will help you develop the skills required to deliver best practice and compliance to your organisation. They will also enhance your career by providing you with industry standard certifications and increased peer recognition. Our range of courses offer a structured learning path from foundation to advanced level in the key topics of information security, IT governance, business continuity and service management.

ISO/IEC 20000 is the first international standard for IT service management and has been developed to reflect the best practice guidance contained within the ITIL framework. Our ISO20000 Foundation and Practitioner training courses are designed to provide delegates with a comprehensive introduction and guide to the implementation of an ISO20000 management system and an industry recognised qualification awarded by APMG International. We also have a unique ITIL Foundation (2 day) training course designed to provide delegates with the knowledge and skills required to pass the EXIN ITIL Foundation examination at the very first attempt. This classroom course has been specifically designed to ensure delegates acquire the ITIL Foundation certificate at the lowest cost and with the least time away from the office.

Full details of all IT Governance training courses can be found at *www.itgovernance.co.uk/training.aspx*.

Professional Services and Consultancy

Our expert ITSM consultants can help you to focus on what is really important in service management, highlighting both the relationships that matter and the results that you can influence. The outcome of adopting our recommended management good practice will be process improvements that lead to higher ROI.

We show you how to identify and document process lifecycles in a way that is central to ITSM. Consultancy advice, mentoring and coaching will result in you wasting less time and effort on things that ultimately do not matter. You will also learn through engagement with our consultants and trainers how to consider the effects of your behaviours on those you are connected to, and work productively to influence their decisions and actions.

To quote Roger Williams: 'Achievement does not normally happen by accident. It starts with a clear vision of what success looks like.' Make your project work from day one by drawing on the combined experience of IT Governance's ITSM consultants.

For more information about consultancy from IT Governance Ltd, see: *www.itgovernance.co.uk/consulting.aspx*.

Newsletter

IT governance is one of the hottest topics in business today, not least because it is also the fastest moving.

You can stay up to date with the latest developments across the whole spectrum of IT governance subject matter, including; risk management, information security, ITIL and IT service management, project governance, compliance and so much more, by subscribing to ITG's core publications and topic alert emails.

Simply visit our subscription centre and select your preferences: *www.itgovernance.co.uk/newsletter.aspx*.

EU for product safety is Stephen Evans, The Mill Enterprise Hub, Stagreenan,
Drogheda, Co. Louth, A92 CD3D, Ireland. (servicecentre@itgovernance.eu)